"A great book that provides deep insights into struggle. Let Jamie Smart show you the way."

Jason Bates, Co-founder Monzo

"Jamie does a terrific job of bringing the principles behind the human experience to light in a way that is both illuminating and entertaining. He builds a convincing case that we are indeed in the midst of a paradigm shift in our understanding of who we are and how we can realise our fullest potential."

Ian Watson, Transformational Educator

"Jamie has written a classic book that is revolutionary in its simplicity. I have bought the original version of this book many times for clients, and I'm sure I will be buying copies of this updated edition for many years to come."

Ankush Jain, Author of *Sweet Sharing:*
Rediscovering the REAL You

"I am incredibly excited about the release of the second edition of *Clarity*. If you have read the first edition and thought it was game-changing, then you have to read this one. Its evolution over the past 10 years has pushed it to new heights in terms of its high-value insights into taking ownership of your life. Jamie has a special gift of breaking down complex concepts into easily digestible pieces, making them useful and actionable. If you're looking for a transformative guide to reclaiming your clarity, resilience and well-being, then *Clarity* is an essential read – I highly recommend it."

Dr Rani Bora, Holistic Psychiatrist, Mental Wealth Coach
and Author of *How to Turn Stress on Its Head*

"Take time to go through this book because it is packed with profound insights that will equip you with a deeper understanding of how the mind works and demonstrate how you already have what you need to transform your life."

Simon Alexander Ong, Author of *Energize*

"The first edition of *Clarity* literally changed my life in a 'nothing's-ever-going-to-be-the-same-again' kind of way. Is it possible that this life-changing book just became even more clear? It is. The 2nd edition reflects Jamie's ever-deepening understanding of the principles behind clarity; revisiting this newly updated work is a delight. This book is certain to bring abundant, life-enhancing insight to the open-minded reader."

Mamoon Yusaf, Author of *Inside the Soul of Islam*

"The original version of Jamie Smart's *Clarity* was one of the books I most often recommended to clients and friends, and this newly revised and empowered version is even more enlightening and liberating. A psychological classic for the ages!"

Steve Chandler, Author of *Time Warrior*

"The only personal development book you'll ever need."

Andy Cope, Ph.D., Author of *Shine and The Art of Being Brilliant*

What People Said About the First Edition of *Clarity*

"Jamie Smart takes an outdated paradigm of success and turns it on its head. Pull up a chair, get a copy of *Clarity* and discover how you can experience an exponential increase in clarity and quality of life."

Rich Litvin, Founder of 4PC and Co-author of *The Prosperous Coach*

"Take your time reading this profound book. Jamie Smart is about to blow apart every circumstantial excuse you ever came up with. He's about to put the steering wheel back in your hands."

Garret Kramer, Founder of Inner Sports and
Author of *Stillpower* and *The Path of No Resistance*

"The insights you'll get whilst reading *Clarity* will resonant in how you manage day to day but, more importantly, provide a framework for refreshing your priorities, goals and drive."

Peter Lake, Group Business Development Director, JS Group

"The world of leadership, sales and customer engagement has changed radically over the past ten years. People are more savvy, better informed and sick of the same old story. Jamie Smart cuts through the noise of the marketplace and shows you what really works. Profound, practical and instantly applicable; *Clarity* is essential reading if you want to make your mark in the 21st century."

Paul Charmatz, Former Managing Director, Camelot

"Jamie, you really hit the bullseye with this brilliant book; it's a must-read for everyone who wants clarity of mind."

Joe Stumpf, Founder of By Referral Only and Author of *Willing Warrior*

"Jamie Smart is *brilliant*! In his book *Clarity*, he has unlocked an insight into the real-life matrix. Be ready to have your world turned inside-out because, as Jamie so effortlessly demonstrates, *this* is how it works."
Richard Enion, Founder of Enrichd Superfoods and
Co-founder of Dragon's Den winner, BassToneSlap.com.

"At last – a book that explains the importance of understanding the nature of thought and how the answers are on the inside! I fully endorse and share Jamie's vision for the 'Thought Revolution'."
Andy Gilbert, Founder & developer of
the Go M.A.D.® Thinking System

"Jamie Smart writes in a way that speaks directly to the challenges people face in today's business environment. I'm buying a copy for all my clients."
Cheryl Bond, Ed.D., President, Essential Resilience

"*Clarity* is an amazing book that provides you with the one realization you need to find happiness, wisdom and clarity in life. I highly recommend this book to anyone trying to deal with life stressors and find true wisdom and well-being."
Mark Howard, Ph.D., Clinical Psychologist, ThreePrinciplesInstitute.org

"*Clarity* is an utterly engaging and powerful book that brilliantly elucidates what is undoubtedly *the* most important revolution in psychology. Jamie shares his understanding using a multitude of real-world examples that bring this understanding to life without jargon or hype."
Chantal Burns, Founder of the Conscious Leadership
School and Author of *Instant Motivation*

"Jamie Smart has been a master of life change for many years now, but this is an incredible, perhaps the ultimate, expression of his already powerful wisdom. It's quite simply revolutionary."
Alex West, Co-Executive Producer of the original
BBC TV series *Who Do You Think You Are?*

"This book is the kick up the backside the self-help and success genre so badly needs. A word of warning – this book is very different!"
Simon Hazeldine, Author of *Neuro-Sell*,
International Speaker, Performance Consultant

"If you want real leverage and creativity in your life, read this book."
Catherine Casey M.A., Clinical Psychology,
Principle-Based Consultant, San Jose, California

"*Clarity* is awesome. 500 words in and I was on fire and it didn't stop. . . And what was particularly pleasant was it felt good. Do what every high-performer or entrepreneur looking for modern solutions to live a better life should do: get *Clarity*."

James Lavers, Media Psychologist

"This new understanding not only gave more creativity and success when I was in a good place, it also gives me important insight at other, arguably more important, times. It's massively valuable in my success as modern day businessman."

Julian Freeman, Entrepreneur

"*Clarity* is thought-provoking and profound – a radical and yet common-sense approach to change, leadership and personal development."

Amanda Menahem, HR Director, Hastings Direct

"Brilliant! *Clarity* is packed with inspiration, epiphanies and eurekas on every page. Jamie Smart teaches that clarity is our natural state, and that when we get clear about who we are and about how life works, it helps us to be happier, more successful, and more loving men and women."

Robert Holden Ph.D., Author of *Authentic Success,*
Loveability and Higher Purpose

CLARITY

CLARITY

Clear Mind, Better Performance, Bigger Results

Second Edition

Jamie Smart

CAPSTONE
A Wiley Brand

Registered Offices
John Wiley & Sons, Inc., 111 River Street, Hoboken, NJ 07030, USA

Capstone Publishing Ltd. (A Wiley Company), The Atrium, Southern Gate, Chichester, West Sussex, PO19 8SQ, United Kingdom

Editorial Office
The Atrium, Southern Gate, Chichester, West Sussex, PO19 8SQ, UK

For details of our global editorial offices, customer services, and more information about Wiley products visit us at www.wiley.com.

Library of Congress Cataloging-in-Publication Data is Available:

ISBN 9780857089366 (Paperback)
ISBN 9780857089380 (ePDF)
ISBN 9780857089373 (ePub)

Cover Design and Image: Wiley

Set in 10/13pt Sabon by Straive, Chennai, India

SKY10039712_120822

To my daughters,
Matilda and Tallulah

Contents

Preface

Clarity is your mind's natural state. It reflects an innate capacity for resilience, wisdom and well-being that exists within everyone. As the world becomes increasingly complex and uncertain, our need to rely on these inner qualities becomes more and more important. Yet we live at a time when huge numbers of people are being told they *don't* have access to these resources, told they're in situations which render them out of reach, that they've been damaged in some way or that they never had them in the first place.

Fortunately, that's not the case. Your innate capacity for clarity (and the full spectrum of inner resources that accompany it) is your birthright. These pre-existing qualities are built in, as much a part of you as your ability to use your senses. This book is about what clarity is, why it matters and how to get it to work for you.

The first edition of CLARITY was published in 2013. What you are now reading is both a revision and a reworking of that book. So why a 10th anniversary edition and why is it worth reading (even if you read the original)?

The first reason is that the world has changed radically since CLARITY was first published. While the book warned that our mental clarity was under attack, it was written at a time before the effects of social media algorithms and the influence of "big tech" were well understood. The battle for our attention has accelerated exponentially since then, and its impact is all too evident. People have become more polarised and tribal, but *without* the experience of connection and intimacy that comes with genuine belonging. Our sense-making apparatuses are being overwhelmed with information, misinformation and disinformation; it's becoming increasingly difficult to discern the true from the false. As cataclysmic changes sweep through society, people are losing faith in the institutions many used to rely on for their sense of security, purpose and meaning. Perhaps inevitably, a global epidemic of mental health problems is emerging at the very time when we most need the qualities of resilience, wisdom and insight this book is pointing to.

The second reason is that an understanding of the principles behind clarity has made its way into the mainstream. When I first stumbled across these principles, they were psychology's best-kept secret; hardly anyone had heard of this work and even fewer people knew how to share it effectively. I've spent the last 14 years deepening my own understanding and sharing it more widely. I've made videos, done interviews and appeared on TV news. I've spoken at conferences, written books and trained coaches, therapists and business leaders. A few years ago I was in the UK's largest bookseller (WHSmith) and I saw CLARITY and two other principles-based books in the nonfiction bestsellers list. Not long after that, my second book RESULTS became a *Sunday Times* bestseller. These were obvious signs that this understanding was reaching a much wider audience. At the same time, my own understanding has grown simpler and clearer. So ten years have passed and (thanks to the insights and actions of huge numbers of people) the understanding of every individual's innate capacity for clarity, resilience and well-being is on the map. The number of people sharing this understanding has increased significantly and (through them) many people's lives have been transformed.

The third reason is that we're living at a time of enormous potential. A new kind of world is being born, and (like any birth) it's a time of great vulnerability to threats (e.g. artificial intelligence, authoritarianism, climate change, cyberattacks, nuclear war, pandemics, societal collapse, terrorism, etc.). But it also holds great promise, potential and possibility. The popularity of audiobooks, podcasts and video streaming has had a massively democratising effect on education (possibly the biggest innovation in this domain since the invention of the printing press). Digital technology enables us to do things on our devices (e.g. photography, music, banking) that would have taken a truckload of equipment in the past. A search engine gives everyone on the planet access to the kind of information that only the wealthiest in society would have had access to 50 years ago. New possibilities for the monetary system, forms of organisation and even government lie ahead. Exponential technology is providing incredible benefits, but our habits of thinking have not developed for an exponential world. We need to tap into our innate capacities for wisdom, realisation and transformation to meet the challenges of the digital age. We'll also need love, courage and compassion.

Like the original book, this edition aims to answer these questions: *What is clarity? Why is clarity essential? How does clarity work, and how can you get it to work for you? Why do we need clarity now more than ever?* Here are some of the ways this new edition builds on the first edition of CLARITY:

- The book has been updated to reflect the evolution of my own insights and understanding based on an additional ten years of field-testing with individuals and organisations.
- There are new case studies as well as updates on some of the case studies from the original looking at how an understanding of the principles has continued to positively impact the subjects' lives.
- Each chapter has a "What the Research Says" section, linking to journal articles, videos and other materials to help you develop your own evidence base for the material in CLARITY.
- You'll be introduced to *subtractive psychology*, simple but powerful principles that will start clearing your mind automatically and awakening your innate capacities.
- There's also a new chapter, "Troubleshooting Enlightenment," with case studies looking at some of the most common challenges and issues people struggle with (e.g. goals, stress, anxiety, depression, purpose, relationships, etc.).

Thomas Kuhn's groundbreaking book, *The Structure of Scientific Revolutions*, introduced the term "paradigm" to describe the prevailing worldview that underpins a scientific field. A paradigm shift – the superseding of such a worldview – is massively disruptive to normal science. Kuhn explained that a new paradigm opens up ways of perceiving and understanding reality that weren't previously available.

What this edition of *CLARITY* endeavours to describe is a genuinely new paradigm, in the Kuhnian sense. In his fascinating 2002 book, *The Discovery of the Germ* author John Waller says this:

"*. . . a real revolution is something that transforms major aspects of our world and the way we see it. The extraordinary albeit bloodless, scientific revolution that took place between 1880 and 1900 provides us with a paradigmatic example. For in this short space of time, medicine underwent perhaps its greatest ever transformation. In just 20 years, the central role of germs in producing illness was for the first time decisively demonstrated and Western doctors abandoned misconceived ideas about the causes and nature of disease that had persisted, in one form or another, for thousands of years.*"

My assertion is that the principles you're going to be discovering in this book are to psychology what the discovery of germs was to medicine:

. . . a real revolution is something that transforms major aspects of our world and the way we see it. . .

That's what I believe the principles behind clarity represent and why I'm so passionate about sharing them with you. I envision a world where everybody on the planet is aware of their innate capacity for clarity, resilience and well-being. My mission is to awaken people to this capacity and help them awaken others. That's why I've written this book.

I invite you to open to the possibility that major aspects of your world and the way you see it may be about to transform.

To your increasing clarity!

Jamie Smart, November 2022

Introduction

....

*"What information consumes is rather obvious:
it consumes the attention of its recipients."*

Herbert Simon, Economist,
winner of the Nobel Prize
in Economics, 1978

**"If a pond is clouded with mud, there's nothing you can do to
make the water clear. But when you allow the mud to settle,
it will clear on its own, because clarity is the water's natural
state..."**

Clarity is your *mind's* natural state.

For many years, I've been sharing this simple metaphor in
workshops and seminars with business leaders, military personnel,
entrepreneurs, coaches, therapists and private individuals. As people
allow their mud to settle, clarity emerges, and they discover they
have what they need for the job at hand.

So what is clarity, and why does it matter? How does clarity
work, and why do so many people struggle to find it? Most important,
how can you find the clarity you need and start benefiting
from it?

It's well known that outstanding leaders in every field, from Olympic gold medal winners to visionary entrepreneurs, profit from the flow states that a clear mind brings. With clarity of thought comes the qualities that drive sustainable results. These qualities and results are what individuals and organisations are searching for. But, due to *a simple misunderstanding*, we've been looking in the wrong place until now.

The purpose of this book is to clear up that misunderstanding and help you experience greater and greater clarity, with all the benefits it provides. The book asks and answers the following questions:

1. *What is clarity?* It turns out that clarity is a kind of "universal resource." When we have a clear mind, we have everything we need for the job at hand. Ask a nervous speaker what's going through their head when they're onstage, and they'll explain their fears, worries and anxieties. Ask a confident speaker what they're thinking about onstage and the answer's fairly consistent: "Nothing!" This is the case in every field of high performance, from the classroom to the playing field, from the boardroom to the bedroom; when you've got nothing on your mind, you're free to give your best.

2. *Why is clarity essential?* You're going to discover why clarity is so important for living a life that's successful on the *inside* as well as on the outside. It turns out that many of the most desirable qualities people struggle to "develop" (such as resilience, creativity, motivation, intuition, confidence and even leadership) are actually expressions of an innate capacity; they're emergent properties of an uncluttered mind. These qualities drive the results people desire. Clarity is the source of authentic leadership and high performance. It allows us to be present in the moment and have an enjoyable experience of life. A sense of purpose, direction and entrepreneurial spirit are natural for people with a clear head. So are happiness, freedom, security, love, confidence and peace of mind.

3. *How does clarity work, and how can you get it to work for you?* You're going to be introduced to *subtractive psychology*,

simple but powerful principles that will start clearing your mind *automatically* and awakening your innate qualities. These are the principles behind the natural capacity for experience – thinking, feeling and perceiving – every person is born with. This innate capacity generates 100% of our experience of life, moment to moment.

Clarity is a naturally emergent property of this capacity – it isn't something you *do*; it's something you already *have*. The mind has its own "self-clearing" function, capable of guiding you back to clarity, regardless of what state (or circumstances) you're in. Although this is extremely evident in small children, all but a fortunate few have it conditioned out of their awareness by the time they reach adulthood.

As you start to deepen your understanding of the principles behind clarity, you're going to reconnect with your mind's natural self-clearing function. As a result, you'll find that you start having (a) an effortlessly clear mind, (b) more time for what's important, (c) improved decision-making, (d) better performance where it counts, and (e) more of the results that matter to you. Some of the "side effects" you may notice include better relationships, reducing stress levels, more passion and an increasing engagement with life.

4. *Why do we need clarity now, more than ever?* We're living at a pivotal time in history; millions of people are faced with uncertainty, complexity and overwhelm. As individuals, as organisations and as an entire species, clarity is the key to solving the big issues that face us if we want to create a sustainable future for ourselves and the generations that follow us.

All of which presents us with a serious challenge: As our world becomes increasingly uncertain, complex and chaotic, we seem to have less and less time, attention and wisdom to navigate it with.

At a point in history when we most need clarity, it appears to be in shorter and shorter supply. . .

And so we try to compensate, as individuals and as organisations. From time management to mindfulness, from speed-reading to positive thinking, we try to get back in control. And at first, it *looks* like it's helping; we *feel* like we're back in the driving seat. But then we lose motivation, or forget to use the technique; our attention gets drawn elsewhere or we fail to apply what we've learned.

It's not working. And it's not your fault.

You see, without even realising it, we've been using an industrial-age *misunderstanding* of how the mind works to try to deal with the challenges of a digital-age world. This misunderstanding gives rise to the contaminated thinking (e.g. worry, anxiety, overthinking, etc.) that obscures our innate capacity for peace, presence, high performance, creativity, confidence, security and love. As you start to see through the misunderstanding, clarity will emerge more and more frequently and reliably. To put it succinctly: *Clarity equals capacity minus contamination.*

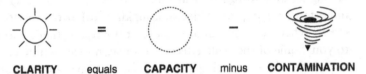

CLARITY equals **CAPACITY** minus **CONTAMINATION**

As you continue reading this book, you're going to start dissolving the conditioning that's been keeping you from clarity until now and notice yourself experiencing a clear mind more and more frequently (with all the benefits it brings). At the times when your mind *is* clouded, you'll know what to do (and more important, what *not* to do). The conditioning is based in three main areas:

1. *Contaminated thinking arising from the outside-in misunderstanding.* A widespread piece of conditioning mistakenly attributes clarity (and the lack of it) to a variety of circumstances. While this can easily be shown not to be the case, the misunderstanding is extremely persistent when it goes unchallenged. As your understanding of the principles behind clarity starts deepening, you'll notice stale habits of contaminated thinking dropping away and clarity emerging to take their place.

2. *The move from a manufacturing economy to a knowledge economy.* Just as factory workers need to keep their machines clean and well-oiled, knowledge workers, creatives, coaches, entrepreneurs managers and leaders need to take similar care of their minds. Individuals and businesses are paying the price as time scarcity, attention poverty and information saturation clog the "mental machinery" we rely on. But there's good news. People are born with a powerful immune system that protects us from disease and illness. The immune system reflects an innate tendency towards health and wellness that also shows up in the body's ability to repair wounds, breaks and other injuries. It is a little-known fact, however, that people also have a *psychological* immune system, able to quickly restore even an extremely perturbed mind to clarity and well-being.

As your understanding of the principles behind clarity continues to deepen, you'll find that you have what you need to prosper in times of uncertainty, complexity and change.

3. *Attempting to find clarity using outside-in methods.* The mind is a self-correcting system. The primary condition needed for a self-correcting system to find its way back to balance is simple: an absence of external interference. Outside-in methods such as positive thinking, affirmations and other techniques can often be examples of external interference. Other examples include smoking, drinking too much and internet addiction. While they can be used to find relief in the short term, they are not a sustainable solution. In the long run, they often make matters worse if they give the busy-minded person even *more* to think about and do (I'm assuming that the *last* thing you need is more on your mind).

Subtractive psychology: less is more

As you read this book, there's nothing you need to do, think about or implement. . .

- You won't need new regimes, systems or processes to remember.

- You won't be given lists of techniques, tactics or interventions to put into practice.
- You won't have to reframe, monitor or manage your thinking.

This book is designed to *effortlessly* activate your innate capacity for clarity. As you'll find out, the principles you're going to be discovering will take care of the implementation for you.

Reality Check

"Seriously?" I hear you ask. *"While I love the idea that my life could get better just by reading a book, it sounds way too good to be true. How's that supposed to work?"*

Great question! Here's how I explained it in my book *RESULTS*:

Most approaches for creating results are additive, giving you theories, techniques and concepts to remember, practise and apply. While additive approaches are often compelling, they rarely yield the desired results (for reasons we'll explore later). Fortunately, the understanding you're going to be developing as you read this book is subtractive. Instead of giving you more to remember, the principles you're going to be learning will take things off your mind, giving you less to think about. As a result, you're going to have a clear mind more of the time and more space for the endeavours and experiences that matter.

DISTINCTION: Acting It versus Catching It

If you've ever pretended to have a cold (perhaps while phoning in to work), you'll know that it's not that easy and not very convincing. It's tough to fake a sneeze, never mind the other unpleasant symptoms. This is an example of **acting it**. Most business and personal development books aim at giving you the things to think, change and do so you can "act" in a certain way to get the results you want.

However, when you actually *have* a cold, the symptoms emerge effortlessly. They're entirely convincing because they're *real*. This is an example of **catching it**. This book is designed so that you can "catch" an understanding that's more closely aligned with how your mind (and life) really works. As you catch the understanding, it will spontaneously result in the "symptoms" of increasing clarity, resilience and peace of mind, with all the other qualities and behaviours that naturally proceed from those states.

For this reason, the book has been designed differently from a traditional business or personal development book. It doesn't contain lists of things to do, and doesn't attempt to be coolly objective. Instead, it includes

- Distinctions clarifying important points
- Simple thought experiments you can conduct in under a minute
- Mini case studies from the experiences of my corporate and personal clients
- Real-world stories as well as numerous metaphors and analogies
- Scientific explanations expressed in down-to-earth terminology
- Examples from history, current events and popular culture
- Personal details and anecdotes from my own life
- Reality checks where necessary
- Diagrams and illustrations

While you may find yourself reading this book again and again, you don't have to work at it. You're going to start seeing that you have a lot more going for you than you may have realised until now. One suggestion: This book is cumulative; Part Two and Part Three have plenty of interesting case studies and examples, but they will not make much sense until you've read Part One. Your first time through, I strongly encourage you to read this book from the beginning.

It may sound like a bold claim, but the understanding you're going to be exposed to is, quite literally, effortless. The changes you can expect to see as you start to get a feel for these principles share three important qualities:

- Your changes will be *natural*, a perfect fit to who you are.
- Your changes will be *sustainable*; it's time to say goodbye to struggle and backsliding.
- Your changes will be *generative*. This means that the positive impact of what you'll be learning will show up in many different aspects of your life, without you having to "make it happen."

As you read this book, you may be struck by the universal nature of what you're learning. People are often stunned that no one has ever told them this before. Paradoxically, they also remark that they've always known this on some level. As you start to experience the profound impact of increasing clarity in your own life, you may start to notice yourself feeling more optimistic and hopeful for your fellow human beings. Clarity is our best bet if we are to meet the challenges of our rapidly changing world and leave a sustainable legacy for the generations to come.

But that's for later. The first step is for you to start discovering just how much *more* you've got going for you than you've previously imagined (even if you already know you've got a lot going for you). I want to assure you that you have the capacity for sustainable clarity and all the benefits it brings. But first, a question:

Q: If you're caught in a trap, what's the one thing you have to do before you can escape?
A: You have to realise that you've been caught in a trap.

Until you realise you've been caught in a trap, you're very unlikely to get out of it. But once you know about the trap, and you can see how it works, then escape is pretty straightforward. Especially if other people have escaped from the same trap and can show you how.

So please allow me to reveal the trap that's ensnared millions of people, including me. . .

keep exploring ⁘ connect with others
share your discoveries ⁘ deepen your understanding

At the end of each chapter, you'll find a section containing three elements:

Thought Experiment: *This is a statement or question for reflection to help you integrate what you're learning even more deeply. For example:*

Thought Experiment: We each experience greater clarity from time to time. As you look back now, what are some of the more memorable occasions when you've found yourself experiencing an unexpected increase in clarity?

When you reach a thought experiment, pause for a moment. You don't have to figure out the question or "get it right." You don't even have to answer it. Just reading the question and reflecting on it for a moment is enough to continue your process of integration.

What the Research Says: This is a description of (and where possible, a link to) peer-reviewed articles and other research that will help you "read around" the principles behind clarity. Because these principles aren't yet part of the scientific mainstream, most research won't refer directly to them. Nevertheless, each of these research elements will help you join the dots as you establish your own personal evidence base for what you're learning.

Additional Resources: This section will also contain a website URL to enter into your browser and a QR code you can scan. These will take you to web pages containing other material relating to the chapter you've just read, ranging from videos and audio recordings to articles, photos and infographics. Experience shows that sharing your discoveries is a simple but powerful way for you to continue integrating what you're learning, as your understanding of the principles behind clarity continues to deepen. I encourage you to share what you're learning with others as you make your way through the book.

www.JamieSmart.com/ClarityIntro

PART ONE

The Essential Foundations

1

Misunderstanding: The Hidden Trap

....

*"None are more hopelessly enslaved than those
who falsely believe they are free."*

Johann Wolfgang von Goethe
Poet, playwright, novelist
and philosopher

**"An addict is someone who's trying to use a *visible* solution to
solve an *invisible* problem. . ."**

I was no stranger to addiction when I heard this. I started drinking
when I was 12 years old and didn't stop for good until I was 30.
On the journey of recovery, my life improved in ways that I didn't
even imagine were possible. But, in the process, I discovered an even
deeper addiction at the very heart of modern culture. This addiction
is so subtle, it's almost *invisible*, a life-eroding trap that has hooked
countless millions of people. . .

The hidden hamster wheel

The hidden hamster wheel is one of the most common barriers to clarity. It's based in a misunderstanding that's taken to be "obviously true" by most people. It's so subtle and pervasive that it shows up in everything from children's books to leadership programmes, from movies to marketing campaigns.

The Power of Misunderstanding

In the 1800s, it was widely accepted that illnesses such as cholera and the plague were caused by "bad air" (also known as atmospheres or miasmas). At the time, huge numbers of people were moving to Soho in London, with an associated increase in sewage. The council of the day decided to dump the excess waste into the river Thames, unknowingly contaminating the water supply, and causing a cholera outbreak that claimed the lives of 618 Soho residents in just a few weeks.

The miasma theory was a misunderstanding that was seen as fact. As a result, the decision to pump sewage into the water supply was taken from within that misunderstanding. While you and I know it's crazy to let human waste into your drinking water supply, that's because we have a better understanding of reality.

Misunderstanding can lead to needless misery, suffering and even death. But as soon as people get a clearer understanding of the nature of reality *as it already is,* there can be a massive and widespread improvement in quality of life.

Thought Experiment

Imagine this: It's 1853, you live in Soho, London. It's a crowded city, with only rudimentary sanitation. The air is full of strong odours, so you're in the habit of carrying a posy, a small bunch of flowers to protect you from illness. Everyone you know does the same thing, and the posy industry is big business.

Then one day you meet a scientist who's convinced diseases *aren't* caused by bad smells. He tells you disease is actually transmitted by tiny invisible creatures, but when you ask for evidence, he explains that we don't currently have the equipment that could show you the little creatures (or "germs" as he calls them). He tells you, however, that he can show you phenomena that can only be explained by the existence of these germs.

Would you believe it? Maybe, maybe not. Most people would probably say *"Don't be silly – everybody knows that illness is caused by bad smells. It's obvious. . ."*

My guess is that until I had some compelling evidence to the contrary, I'd be tempted to keep buying posies, and so would you.

An essential question

If you were to be presented with the evidence that one of the most widely held beliefs of modern society was in fact a misunderstanding about how life works, would you be able to listen with an open mind? The fact that you're reading this means the answer is probably "yes," so here goes. . .

The life-damaging misunderstanding that I call the *hidden hamster wheel* is the mistaken belief that our "core states" such as security, confidence, peace, love, happiness and success can be provided or threatened by past, present or future circumstances, by something "visible."

We have this belief because we've been conditioned to believe that there's somewhere to get to, and that "there" is better than "here." And "there" comes in a variety of tantalising flavours that look something like this:

I'll be *[happy/secure/fulfilled/peaceful/better/successful/ok]* when I. . .

- Find the right work/hobby/partner/community – the "there" of doing and relationships
- Get the money/write the book/start the business/lose the weight – the "there" of accomplishment

- Change my thinking/my limiting beliefs/do my affirmations – the "there" of mindset
- Meditate properly/find the right practice/get enlightened – the "there" of spirituality

I know, because I've done it – virtually everything on this list and more. I got value from many of my efforts, but sooner or later, after a week or a month or a year, I'd find myself feeling in some ways like I was back where I started, feeling like there was something missing, something wrong, something I couldn't quite put my finger on. . .

As it turns out, the story behind that sense of "something missing" doesn't just stop people from enjoying their lives to the full – it often stands in the way of having the life you *truly* want. You see, as strange as it may sound, we've fallen into a trap. And it's a trap that's so subtle, most of us have never even noticed it. Subtle, powerful and all-pervasive.

The "*I'll be happy when. . .*" trap is an example most people can identify with. The core states and circumstances vary, but the basic structure of the superstition is the same:

I'll be [*core state*] when I have [*circumstance*].

It's based on an even simpler structure:

[*circumstance*] causes [*core state*].

And like pieces of Lego, this simple structure can be used to assemble all kinds of larger structures:

- I couldn't be [*core state*] if I lost [*circumstance*].
- I'm [*core state*] because of [*circumstance*].
- I can't be [*core state*] because I don't have [*circumstance*].
- I was [*core state*] until I lost [*circumstance*].
- I'm convinced that [*core state*] comes from [*circumstance*].

They can take a variety of shapes, but at heart they're all based on the idea that our felt experience of life comes from something relatively visible.

You may have seen studies that show that feelings of well-being and high self-esteem come from accomplishments or from doing vocational work or from meditating. But that's all an example of the misunderstanding in action. When I use the word "circumstance," I'm using it in the widest possible way to refer to pretty much anything you can imagine (and at any point in time, past, present and future) for instance:

- Physical environment (e.g. home, holiday destination, working environment)
- What a person does (e.g. work, hobbies, exercise)
- Techniques (e.g. meditation, neuro-linguistic programming [NLP] state change, emotional freedom technique [EFT] tapping)
- Stuff (e.g. houses, boats, cars)
- Status (e.g. job title, position, medals)
- Material wealth (e.g. money, shares, income)
- People (e.g. partners, friends, children)
- And so on

The idea that our core states are at least to some degree the result of our circumstances seems so obvious to people that calling it into question can seem ridiculous at first.

And while many people who have explored the domains of "brain change" (through NLP, spirituality, personal development, meditation, etc.) would say that they "know" that their core states don't come from their circumstances, their behaviour often suggests that they don't really know it ("I know that intellectually but. . .").

In fact, people often replace one set of circumstances with a "higher level" version of the same thing. . .

- I'll be happy when I change my limiting beliefs.
- I'll feel fulfilled when I know that I'm on purpose and doing work I love.

- I'll be on track once I become an authentic leader.
- I'll feel secure when I'm generating passive income.
- I'll feel a sense of freedom when I have the lifestyle I want.
- I'll be OK when I go on the next course/read the book/do the exercises and so on.

The circumstances may be different but the superstitious structure is still in place:

[*circumstance*] causes [*core state*].

Once again: We've been conditioned to believe that our clarity, security and well-being come from the *outside*, that there's somewhere to get to, and that "there" is better than "here."

Reality Check

"Don't be silly!" I hear you say. "Everybody knows that circumstances give us feelings. I'll give you some examples right now. . .

- *My sense of security comes from the fact that I've got a good job and money in the bank.*
- *I feel a sense of love and connection because I've found the right partner.*
- *I feel stressed out because I've got a stressful business.*
- *I feel peaceful when I go for a walk in the park.*
- *I feel relaxed when I go on holiday.*

Are you really trying to tell me that these examples aren't real? That my work doesn't actually stress me out? That my security doesn't come from money? That I don't feel love because of my partner? That I don't like going on holiday?"

Yes and no.

Your examples of your experience are real for you. I'm sure you can identify numerous situations where you reliably feel a certain way. I'm not saying you don't enjoy the things you enjoy or that you shouldn't want the things that you want. What I'm saying is that the feelings aren't the result of the circumstances – they're coming from something else entirely. And, as you start to understand where they're coming from, and how the system works, some wonderful things can start to happen.

But I'm getting ahead of myself.

These days, I experience more clarity than I ever thought possible, with all the considerable benefits it brings. But I didn't get here in the way you might expect.

In brief: I grew up in an alcoholic household and started drinking heavily when I was 12 years old. By age 19, I was a scholarship engineering student and a full-blown alcoholic. The alcohol was like rocket fuel for my life: I got jobs, was promoted rapidly, and started experiencing many of the trappings of success – expense accounts, foreign travel, luxurious surroundings – but on the inside, I was slowly falling apart.

At the age of 30 I got married. A month later, her bags were packed so I decided to stop drinking in order to save my marriage.

Oh yeah – I missed one. I'll be happy when I get a cigarette/a drink/a line of coke – the "there" of *addiction*.

That was in 1996, and I haven't had a drink since. Today I live a fulfilling life that's beyond anything I dreamed was possible for me, but how I got here is a story of struggle, frustration and heartbreak (much of which I could have avoided if I'd known what you're going to be discovering in this book).

Just to give you an idea, in the time period from 1996 to 2008 I . . .

- Got married, had two children and moved to London.
- Managed multimillion-pound projects and became fascinated with the process of how people and organisations change.
- Was paralysed by a combination of fear of failure and fear of success (I felt like I was a fraud, always worrying that I'd be "found out").
- Read hundreds of personal development books and went on dozens of personal development courses.
- Quit my job and became a consultant, doing strategy workshops, teambuilding, executive coaching and training.
- Tried my hand at stand-up comedy and overcame my fear of public speaking (mainly by doing lots of public speaking).
- Lost weight, gained weight, lost weight, gained weight, lost weight, gained weight.

- Spent countless hours talking to a Freudian psychoanalyst and participated in various addiction recovery programmes.
- Learned NLP, built a successful training company and grew a tribe of many tens of thousands of people who follow my work.
- Was left by my wife, and struggled with worry, anxiety, depression and suicidal thoughts.
- Had numerous false horizons, thinking I'd finally "got it," only to find myself feeling like I was back where I started.

By the end of 2008, I was unhappy, stressed out and at the end of my tether. I felt like I'd been giving it everything I had for over a decade, and while some areas of my life were better than ever, in many ways I felt like I'd been running on the spot. While I had many of the *trappings* of success (passive income, time freedom, foreign travel, etc.), I wasn't having a *feeling* of success. I was on the verge of giving up.

Then I was introduced to the understanding you're going to be discovering in this book. As I write the second edition, it's 14 years on, and they've been the best years of my life. I'm experiencing a sense of clarity, peace, security, love and aliveness unlike anything I've had before. As my level of understanding has continued to increase, my relationships, results and external circumstances have been improving too. And the good news is that it can be replicated. My clients are getting similar results:

- Less stress, more clarity and peace of mind
- More creative and innovative, finding solutions to problems more easily
- Better working relationships and more harmony in their personal lives
- More productive individuals and teams, getting more done and having more free time
- Better business results and better performance where it counts
- Fears, anxieties and limitations falling away effortlessly
- Natural motivation, making real progress with the things that matter
- Better health, with more vibrancy and aliveness

It's working for them, so it can work for you, because seeing through a misunderstanding can give you a disproportionate increase in the results you get. Why? Because a misunderstanding is just a piece of flawed logic, a perception that often leads to unwanted. . .

- Stress
- Pressure
- Poor productivity
- Dissatisfaction
- Conflict
- Worry
- Anxiety

- Irritation
- Frustration
- Resentment
- Addiction
- Mental illness
- Depression
- Burnout

- Divorce
- Poverty
- Bullying
- Criminality
- Violence
- And so on

But the great news is that the moment an individual starts to wake up from this misunderstanding, their quality of life starts to get better and better.

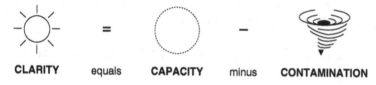

CLARITY   equals   **CAPACITY**   minus   **CONTAMINATION**

So how do you escape from this addictive, life-damaging trap? How do you start to dissolve the misunderstanding, and begin to experience an enormous increase in clarity and quality of life (even if it's already great)?

---

keep exploring ⁘ connect with others
share your discoveries ⁘ deepen your understanding

Thought Experiment: *We all fall into the "I'll be happy when. . ." trap from time to time. As you reflect on your life so far, what are some of the ways you now realise you've been accidentally hoodwinked by this illusion until now?*

What the Research Says: The classic paper "Lottery Winners and Accident Victims: Is Happiness Relative?" was published in the *Journal of Personality and Social Psychology* in 1978 and has been cited over 3700 times.

Three groups were studied: (1) people who had wins on the lottery of between $50,000 and $1,000,000, (2) people who had been seriously injured in accidents and rendered paraplegic or quadriplegic, and (3) a control group. The study found that "lottery winners were not happier than controls and took significantly less pleasure from a series of mundane events." The accident victims "exhibited a strong nostalgia effect, rating their past as much happier than did controls."

The study's authors drew the conclusion that people tend to "overestimate the overall magnitude and generality of the positive or negative feeling generated by an event."

Brickman, P., Coates, D., & Janoff-Bulman, R. (1978). Lottery winners and accident victims: Is happiness relative? *Journal of Personality and Social Psychology, 36*(8), 917–927.

You can access the paper at www.JamieSmart.com/research/Clarity1

Additional Resources

www.JamieSmart.com/Clarity1

2

The Power
of Insight

....

*"We cannot teach people anything; we can only
help them discover it within themselves."*

Galileo Galilei Astronomer,
physicist and mathematician

**"Don't take this the wrong way, but I get the impression that
you haven't been listening very well until now. . ."**

I thought I was a *great* listener, but my coach explained that when
I was listening, it seemed like I had a lot on my mind. Listening
was something I was *working* at. He said that listening in this way
was fine for getting an intellectual understanding of something, but
it wasn't going to help me have the clarity and insights that could
make a real and lasting difference in my life.

As I reflected on it, I realised that this is how we've *all* been
taught to listen. It's how we've been taught to *read*. It's how we've
been "taught" to *learn*.

But it used to be different.

You were born a listener and learner. It's thanks to these natural abilities that you can walk and talk today. Then, we were taught to read, listen and learn for an *intellectual* understanding. But it's time to remember a different way to read, listen and learn. . .

DISTINCTION: Reading for Information versus Reading for Realisation

- **Reading for information:** When most people read, they're looking to verify and build on what they know. When we read for information, we think about what we're reading as we're reading it, making decisions about (1) whether or not we agree with it, (2) where it fits into our existing cognitive structures, (3) if it doesn't fit, why not?, (4) whether to accept or reject it, (5) if/ how we're going to apply it, and so on. A person who's reading for information has "something on their mind," so the mind isn't free to do what it does best – generate fresh, clear thinking.

- **Reading for insight:** When you're reading for insight, you're creating space for an intuitive knowing that already exists within your consciousness to emerge more fully into your awareness. Reading for insight is reading with nothing on your mind. When you read for an insight, you put your existing conceptual models to one side and allow yourself to be impacted by what you're reading.

When it comes to clarity, reading for information is like drinking salt water; it just makes you more thirsty. . .

The Magic Eye

In the 1990s, evolving technology led to the creation of "magic eye" images. At first glance, a magic eye image looks like a repeating, two-dimensional pattern, but if you look through the image, with a soft-eyed, relaxed gaze, a 3D figure suddenly leaps into your awareness.

People often sat staring at the 2D images, trying hard to see the 3D image hidden within it, but nothing happened until they relaxed and allowed the image to emerge.

Reading for realisation is sort of like looking at a magic eye picture. You don't really need to think about what you're reading – you just relax and allow yourself to be impacted by the words. The insight that can clear your mind and give you fluid, fresh realisations isn't in the words anyway; it's a capacity that's right there inside of you, preloaded into your consciousness.

Another example is music. When you listen to music you enjoy, you're not trying to decide whether you agree with it or not. You're listening to be impacted, to enjoy it and have an experience. When you're reading or listening for realisation, you get a feel for what the person's saying, seeing beyond the written (or spoken) word to what the author's really trying to convey. You're making space for an insight to emerge from within *your* consciousness (this is what's happening when you get a sudden "a-ha").

The Power of Realisation

To get a feel for the difference between *intellectual* understanding and *insightful* understanding, imagine a dog that's constantly chasing his tail. Now let's imagine that the dog hires you and me as consultants to help him with overall productivity. We ask the dog what he needs, and he says something like this:

Here's what I need: First, I need more speed, because the thing I'm chasing is very fast. It always seems to be able to outrun me. Second, I need more agility, because this thing is also very nimble. Even when I creep up on it, it manages to slip away before I can catch it. Third, I need better strategy, because no matter what I do, it always seems one step ahead of me. It's almost as if it knows what I'm thinking! Finally, I need more time. I'm already working 12-hour days on this, and it just doesn't seem to be enough. So that's what I need: more speed, more agility, better strategy and more time.

You and I both know that all the dog *really* needs is to realise that it's *his own tail* he's been chasing. But if we were to tell him that, there are two ways the dog might respond. If he has a realisation and insightfully understands what we tell him, then he would visibly relax, sigh and maybe even chuckle as he gets it. He might say:

That really makes sense. It's a load off my mind, and it sure explains a lot of things which have been puzzling me until now. It's also taken a lot off my to-do list, and I've suddenly got a lot more space in my diary. I've got to admit, I'm feeling a bit sheepish, but it sure is a relief. Thanks for all the extra time!

However, if the dog had an *intellectual* understanding, but didn't have a realisation, he might say something like this:

Right. So you're telling me that it's my tail. Got it. So I need to remember not to chase it, right? OK. So how do I not chase my tail? Can you just take me through the process?

If the dog said this, we'd know that he hadn't really understood.

The biggest value you're going to get from this book isn't going to come from the information on the *pages* – the biggest value is going to come from the core of *your being*, so allow space for that to happen. You see, there's a way in which this book is a kind of *mirror*; its purpose is for you to glimpse a *reflection* of who you really are and what you've got going for you. The intellectual understanding you already have will still be available when you get to the end of the book, so I invite you to put that to one side and allow yourself to be even more deeply impacted.

The reality is that every person has this source of insight and realisation within them. You have everything you need to bring you to clarity. The power behind the changes you make is going to come from within. As you read this book for a realisation, you may occasionally find yourself feeling particularly clear, calm and peaceful. That sense of clarity can be one of the signs that you're being impacted, so enjoy them when they come and relax when they don't.

And what's so great about realisation?

You innate capacity for realisation is an evolutionary development. Its purpose is entirely practical: to bring our perceptions more closely in alignment with reality. The more aligned with reality you are, the greater your ability to live, survive and thrive. Insightful understanding doesn't come from the words on the page – it comes from the consciousness at the heart of your being. It often arrives suddenly, but it can continue serving and informing you for years to come. Insightful understanding is a natural function of the mind and has the power to make the changes that matter in your life. Realisation is the key to reconnecting you with your mind's self-clearing capacity.

When you read (or listen) for *information*, the intellectual understanding you get is like a written instruction manual; it's good as far as it goes, but it takes effort to put it into practice. That's why people often say *"I understand that intellectually, but. . ."*

A *realisation* is more like an app – once it's downloaded, it starts working immediately; insightful understanding is powered up and ready to go!

Remember in the Introduction when I said there's nothing in this book that you need to do, think about or implement?

- When you have a realisation, it comes with its own source of motivation. You don't need to "get yourself to do it" – you're going to naturally find your behaviour changing in ways that serve you.
- When you have a realisation, it's tailored exactly for you. You don't have to figure it out or try and adjust it to your needs – it already fits you perfectly.
- Insightful understanding is context-sensitive and can adjust to your changing circumstances, even taking account of things you're not consciously aware of.

- Intellectual understandings can get stale over time, but insightful understanding stays fresh and can keep updating your system for years to come.

That's why people so often know what they "should" be doing but don't do it. Until you have a realisation, it's just a nice idea. The great news is that realisations start making a difference to you whether they make sense intellectually or not!

A Sudden Realisation

In the 1990s I was employed as a programme manager, running large organisational change projects for global businesses. After running a number of successful programmes, I wanted to leave my job and become a contractor. My friends assured me I could do it, and while I understood that *intellectually*, I "knew" that I didn't have what it took. Then in 1998 I attended my first personal development training, a two-day programme about the workings of the mind. During the two days, I had a realisation: I suddenly *knew* that I could leave my job and become a contractor, with all the freedom, possibilities and rewards that entailed. I quit my job two weeks later, started working for myself and creating the time and income to follow my passions. I can trace the life I have today back to that realisation and can still feel the sense of freedom and possibility it brought me.

While this example was massively transformational for me, insightful understanding is an everyday phenomenon. In fact, as you start to become more and more aware of it, you'll begin to find yourself relying on realisation and intuition to guide you on a day-to-day basis.

Everyone's had the experience of making a decision, having it turn out badly, then saying *"I knew I should have done it the other way, but I didn't listen to myself."* Many people also have examples of "just knowing" the right thing to do, even though it doesn't seem logical at the time. The intuitive knowing they're referring to is an example of insightful understanding. People have many ways of referring to it:

- The gut feeling that lets you know to take a certain decision
- The common sense that saves the day in a difficult situation
- The intuition that leads you to an unexpected success
- The sudden realisation that makes a big difference in your life
- The "knowing" that has you ask just the right question
- The insight that solves a problem that looked like it was impossible
- The creative leap that takes things in a whole new direction
- The "moment of clarity" that turns an addict's life around
- The inspiration that gives you fresh energy and inner motivation
- The inner wisdom that guides you in situations where your old ideas no longer apply

Most people don't realise how powerful realisation is when it comes to finding clarity, making changes and delivering the goods. And while this book is full of ideas that you may find interesting and informative, its real power is in creating a context where your innate capacity for realisation can give you insightful understanding that makes a real difference in your life.

In fact, the essential difference between this and most other books is this:

The purpose of this book is to act as a catalyst so your own insights and realisations can bring you to clarity, guiding you and helping you make changes as you move forward.

Insightful understanding comes from the principles behind clarity: the source of your innate capacity to have fresh, clear realisations in any moment.

CLARITY equals **CAPACITY** minus **CONTAMINATION**

> **Reality Check**
>
> Sometimes people object, saying that clarity is in fact an *absence* of thought. That is both true and not true. If habitual, stuck patterns of thought are like whitewater rapids, clarity of thought is like the deep, clear waters of a flowing river. That's why so many people who are in the flow say they have nothing on their mind.

Once again, insightful understanding comes from the principles behind clarity, a power that already exists deep within your consciousness. It will show up in ways that can make a difference in your life instantly.

So I invite you to "read for a realisation" as we start exploring a phenomenon that's very strange, entirely counterintuitive and still one of the most shocking things I've ever encountered. . .

---

keep exploring ⁘ *connect with others*
share your discoveries ⁘ *deepen your understanding*

Thought Experiment: *Insights and realisations are a natural part of being alive. Sometimes, small, everyday insights end up being as profound as the big "a-has." As you think about it now, what are some of your more useful and impactful insights and a-ha moments so far?*

What the Research Says: In their 2015 paper, "Psilocybin-occasioned Mystical Experiences in the Treatment of Tobacco Addiction" (310 citations) the researchers used a combination of psilocybin and cognitive behavioural therapy (CBT) for smoking cessation.

Tools used to measure effectiveness included urinalysis, self-reporting and questionnaires. One of these measures – the States of Consciousness Questionnaire (SOCQ) – identified whether participants had a "complete mystical experience" during the psilocybin session, defined as a score of 60% or more on each of the following SOCQ subscales: unity, transcendence of time and space, ineffability, sacredness, noetic quality and positive mood.

The paper's abstract states: "Nine of 15 participants (60%) met criteria for 'complete' mystical experience. Smoking cessation outcomes were significantly correlated with measures of mystical experience on session days, as well as retrospective ratings of personal meaning and spiritual significance of psilocybin sessions. These results suggest a mediating role of mystical experience in psychedelic-facilitated addiction treatment."

Here are some other words for a complete mystical experience: realisation, epiphany, insight.

Garcia-Romeu, A., Griffiths, R. R., Johnson, M. W. (2015). Psilocybin-occasioned mystical experiences in the treatment of tobacco addiction. *Current Drug Abuse Reviews, 7*(3), 157–164.

You can access the paper at www.JamieSmart.com/research/Clarity2

Additional Resources

www.JamieSmart.com/Clarity2

3

How Perception Is Created

....

"Thought creates the world then says 'I didn't do it.'"

David Bohm

"In a dream your mind continuously creates and perceives a world simultaneously . . . so well, that you don't feel your brain doing the creating. . ."

These words are spoken by Leonardo DiCaprio, playing Cobb, in the film *Inception* (2010, Warner Bros. Pictures). He's explaining how dreams work, but our waking experience is generated in exactly the same way (albeit with access to a "live data feed"). To paraphrase Cobb:

In your waking experience of reality, your mind continuously creates and perceives a world simultaneously . . . so well that you don't feel your mind doing the creating.

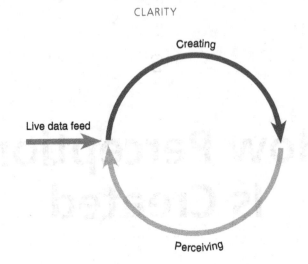

Figure 3.1 Simultaneously Creating and Perceiving

The implications of this can be truly shocking. It means that 100% of your experience of the world "out there" is being generated from within, incorporating data received by the senses to a greater or lesser degree (depending on your focus of attention).

For example, a person can be asleep and dreaming that they're in the front row at a rock concert, only to wake up and discover that the music in their dream was coming from the radio next to their bed. Conversely, a person can be sitting in a business meeting, but have their focus of attention entirely absorbed by a daydream about a future holiday. Whether the data is arriving from your senses, your memories or your imagination, the process that's generating your perceptual experience is the same.

Our experience of reality is, quite literally, created from "the stuff that dreams are made of."

Perceptual Adaptation

The psychologist George Stratton performed a series of intriguing experiments in the 1890s using a pair of "inversion glasses." These curious glasses presented the wearer's eyes with an inverted image of reality – they turned everything upside-down! Stratton himself wore the glasses for eight days straight. For the first four days, he was presented with an upside-down world, but when he woke up on the fifth day of wearing them, something extraordinary had happened; his perception had corrected itself, and he now perceived the world the right way up.

Another surprise followed when he removed the glasses; he found that reality now looked upside down when he *wasn't* wearing them. It was a few days before his sight returned to normal. This phenomenon (referred to as "perceptual adaptation") highlights the creative role the mind plays in generating our moment-to-moment experience of reality.

Stop for a moment. Have a look around you. Listen to any sounds you're aware of. Run your fingers over some objects in your environment. . .

It seems to us as though we look out at the world "out there" through our eyes in much the same way as we look through the viewfinder of a camera, but that's not how it works. The truth of our perception is entirely different and far, far stranger. You see. . .

Our perception of reality is less like looking out at
the world through the lens of a camera and more
like wearing a pair of virtual reality goggles.

Have another look around you and allow yourself to notice one or two objects in your immediate environment. It can be shocking to consider that 100% of your experience of those objects is being generated from within. I know it looks as though the objects are "out there" (and for practical purposes they are "out there") but 100% of your *experience* of the objects is being generated from the consciousness within you. Your entire experience of "out there" is taking place inside of you (including the elements you experience as *outside* of you).

The fabric of your experiential reality is being generated by your mind.

Reality Check

I'm not saying "you create your own reality"; I'm saying that you create your own unique *experience* of reality, moment to moment, from within your consciousness. We live in a material world that is governed by inviolable laws that are not materially influenced by your perception (e.g. gravity, thermodynamics, etc.). If you're walking down the street and fail to notice an uncovered manhole in your path, you're not going to be able to glide over the manhole just because you don't realise it's there. Gravity is a principle, a fundamental law governing our world. As such, it's not bothered about what you or I think!

Energy streams in through all our senses simultaneously as raw data, in much the same way data flow into a computer through a USB port. The mind then creates a model of "what must be

Figure 3.2 Optical Illusion: The Kanisza Triangle

out there for me to be receiving this data." This model is what's "represented" to us in consciousness.

As you look at the Kanisza Triangle, raw data from the image is intercepted by your eyes and transmitted to your brain. Neurological processes enhance the data, filling in the gaps and voila! The perceptual reality generated by your mind includes an illusory white triangle. The brain has a huge variety of these "reality enhancement programmes," developed as survival advantages over countless millennia of evolution (e.g. the ability to discern sharp edges, recognise faces, etc.).

In his fascinating 2005 TED Talk, "Why the Universe Seems So Strange," biologist Richard Dawkins points out that we don't experience the "unvarnished world"; we experience a *model* of the world that's optimised for the type of creature we are, and the kind of world we inhabit. Birds need different kinds of models from monkeys; birds need to be able to deal with aerial navigation, while monkeys need software that allows them to climb trees and swing from branch to branch. Fish need different models from moles or ants, because they inhabit totally different environments and are different types of creature. None of these creatures access the world directly; rather, they live in a mind-made *experiential* reality based on a model or representation that's suited to the type of creature they are and the type of world they inhabit. It's the same with people.

The fabric of your experiential reality is
being generated by your mind.

So what does this have to do with clarity? We'll get there soon, I promise. But first I'd like to share a metaphor with you. . .

The "Pixels" of Perception

As I write, I can see the words I'm typing appearing on the screen of my computer. At any point, I can watch a video, flick through my photos, search on Google or scroll through another document. But one thing remains constant. . .

> *Everything you see on the screen is created using tiny visual building blocks called pixels.*
>
> Similarly, your experience of reality is made of the perceptual equivalent of pixels, an "energy" that I'm going to refer to as the principle of THOUGHT. (I'll use THIS TYPEFACE when I talk about it as a principle.)

Thought Experiment

Look around at the environment you're in. As you notice the different elements in that environment, consider the fact that what you're seeing is actually a representation being generated by (and within) your amazing mind. Your experience of everything you can see is made of the pixels of perception: the power of THOUGHT.

Now close your eyes and remember what you were able to see in your environment. Your memory of those things is also made of THOUGHT.

Now imagine an event you're planning to enjoy in the future. This future memory is made of THOUGHT.

When you're asleep and dreaming, your dreams are made of THOUGHT. Every experience you have in your whole life is generated using the principle of THOUGHT.

Your experience of reality is being created, moment to moment, from within your consciousness, using the power of THOUGHT. . .

The Gherkin and the bell curve

The iconic London skyscraper known as "the Gherkin" gets a variety of responses from people. Some experience it as a shining example of modern architecture; others experience it as a vile monstrosity. If you were to plot 1000 people's subjective experience of the Gherkin, a bell curve would emerge, with a range of responses. For each individual, 100% of their *experience* of the Gherkin would be created from within them, using the power of *THOUGHT*.

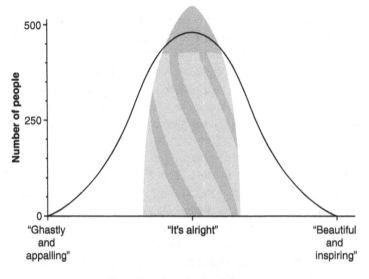

Figure 3.3 The Gherkin Bell Curve

Of course, the energy of THOUGHT isn't just limited to our visual experience. While we've used the visual metaphor of pixels for explanatory purposes, our experiences of sound, smell, taste and touch are also "constructed" from THOUGHT. So are our feelings and emotions.

THOUGHT *is the reality principle.*

It's the power you have to create a representation of absolutely anything and experience it as a reality. We each live in a psychological reality; our perceptual experience is 100% mind-made, using the reality principle, the power of THOUGHT.

Reality Check

If you are scientifically inclined you may be saying to yourself, *"Hang on a second, our perception isn't made of pixels! It's made of synapses, neurons, neurochemicals and electrical currents!"*

Brain science is an incredibly valuable area of research, giving us a close-up view of the "mechanics" of brain functioning. There's no doubt that our brain structures make it possible to perceive in ways that just aren't available to creatures who don't have these structures (for example, the fusiform gyrus, which we use for facial recognition). These brain structures allow us to use THOUGHT in ways that wouldn't be possible without them, but our subjective experience is still created by what I'm calling Thought. In fact, the word THOUGHT itself is just a metaphor for this incredible power.

Here's another way of thinking about it: The London Underground system (aka the Tube) is an incredibly complex network of tunnels, wires and tracks. While the electrical schematics of the underground system have to be incredibly accurate, they're not very useful for finding your way from Oxford Circus to King's Cross. For that, you're better off using the tube map. The Tube map is a masterpiece of simplicity and functionality; incredibly useful for getting from A to B.

If brain chemistry is like the electrician's schematic (accurate, but abstract and very complex), then the principles behind clarity are more like the Tube map – simple, subjective and highly practical once you get the hang of it.

People are literally able to think *anything* and experience it as real. The power of THOUGHT is so flexible that people can use it to create any perceptual reality:

- Two people watching the same movie can have two completely different experiences of it, thanks to THOUGHT.
- A person with a phobia can use the power of THOUGHT to create the experience of an imminent plane crash, a spider bite or a dog attack.
- A person doing a job can feel inspired and energised, while the person sitting next to them feels stressed and unhappy doing *exactly the same work*. Both of them create their experience using THOUGHT.

- A person can become convinced that their business partner is cheating them, regardless of the reality of the situation. They create their perception using THOUGHT, then experience it as real.
- Someone can have a richly enjoyable experience, anticipating a holiday that they're planning to go on. THOUGHT is making that enjoyable experience possible, even if the holiday ends up getting cancelled!

I'm not saying that we're doing this deliberately or consciously. I'm merely pointing to the capacity people have to create literally *any* perception using the incredible power of THOUGHT and then experience that perception as real. This is how our experience is created, and we're using this capacity every moment of our lives.

The reason this is so relevant when it comes to escaping from the hidden hamster wheel and experiencing increasing levels of clarity is this:

100% of our experience of reality is mind-made. If a person believes they need X, Y or Z in order to feel A, B or C, then they will experience that as a reality. That's how powerful THOUGHT is.

Do you remember the structure of the superstition/misunderstanding from Chapter 1?

[circumstance] causes *[core state]*.

THOUGHT has the power to bring each of the different permutations of this contaminated formula to life and have a person experience it as an experiential reality. THOUGHT is like the special-effects department of a movie studio. Its job is to create a perceptual reality that looks, sounds and feels real, regardless of the "facts" of the situation. But we can all think of times when we "knew" something to be true, then later discovered it was an illusion, because. . .

You can't take your THOUGHT-generated perceptual reality at face value – it *always* looks real. That's its job. The sign of high-quality special effects is that you can't tell they're special effects; they look like the real thing!

And THOUGHT is the best special effects department in the world.

So how does knowing this help us? And what does it have to do with clarity?

It turns out that the biggest obstacle to clarity is the result of a kind of "mental magic trick." Like so many magic tricks, its workings have been a secret until now. But it's time to reveal how the trick works. And like any magic trick . . . once you know how the trick is done, it's never the same again. . .

---

keep exploring ❖ connect with others
share your discoveries ❖ deepen your understanding

Thought Experiment: *Take a few moments to look around you. Tune in to whatever sounds you hear and become aware of any tactile sensations you can feel. What happens when you consider the fact that 100% of the experience of your senses is being generated by THOUGHT, moment to moment? That the fabric of your experiential reality "out there" is in fact being generated by your mind?*

What the Research Says: "The World Is Upside Down: The Innsbruck Goggle Experiments of Theodor Erismann (1883–1961) and Ivo Kohler (1915–1985)" is a historical paper published in *Cortex: A Journal Devoted to the Study of the Nervous System and Behavior.*

The article describes George Stratton's original ideas, as well as innovative research done by Erismann and Kohler (the Innsbruck Goggle Experiments of the title). One of the conclusions drawn from the experiments is that "perception isn't a passive process of depicting stimuli that flow in from outside, but a product of constructive, active processes (in which simple sensory processes are directly connected with higher ones, such as those of the memory)."

Sachse, P., Beermann, U., Martini, M., Maran, T., Domeier, M., & Furtner, M. R. (2017). "The world is upside down" – The Innsbruck goggle experiments of Theodor Erismann (1883–1961) and Ivo Kohler (1915–1985). *Cortex, 92,* 222–232.

You can access the paper at www.JamieSmart.com/research/Clarity3

Additional Resources

www.JamieSmart.com/Clarity3

4

The Power of Principles

....

"Misdirection is the art of initiating a train of thought in the mind of the spectator."

Alan Alan
Escapist and illusionist

"It seems as though you've been believing your happiness, security and general OK-ness is dependent on you achieving your goals. . ."

"Yes . . . Obviously!" I replied. I'd just finished explaining to one of my mentors why it was so vitally important that I reach a particular objective.

"That means you don't understand where your security and well-being come from. Your happiness, security and OK-ness doesn't come from outside you, so it's not vulnerable to anything outside you."

I'd fallen for a trick that's been bedevilling people for thousands of years. I'd been fooled into thinking my happiness and well-being were dependent on my circumstances.

DISTINCTION: Inside-out versus Outside-in

- **Inside-out:** We're always living in the feeling of the principle of THOUGHT taking form in the moment. None of our experience is coming from anywhere other than THOUGHT. Our experience of life is less like looking through the viewfinder of a camera and more like wearing a pair of virtual reality goggles. Data streams in through our senses, and we weave it into an experiential reality from the inside-out using the principle of THOUGHT.

- **Outside-in:** Due to a trick of the mind, it often appears as though we're feeling something *other than* the principle of THOUGHT taking form in the moment, like our experience is being created from the outside-in. This illusion can be very compelling, but it never works that way.

History is full of these illusions and false appearances:

Flat Earth versus spherical Earth: People used to believe the Earth was flat, *because that's how it looked to them.* But it was *never* flat; it was always spherical, with some bulging (officially its shape is described as an "oblate spheroid"). It's spherical 100% of the time, even when it looks like it isn't.

Geocentric versus solar-centric: People used to believe the Sun went round the Earth, because that's how it looked to them. But the Sun *never* went round the Earth; the Earth always went round the Sun. The Earth goes round the Sun 100% of the time, even when it looks like it doesn't.

There are two basic mistakes of attribution that people tend to make because of the outside-in misunderstanding:

Mistake 1: We tend to mistakenly attribute our uneasy, unpleasant feelings to something other than the principle of THOUGHT taking form in the moment. But our uneasy, unpleasant, agitated feelings are THOUGHT-generated; they only ever come from within.

Examples:

- I feel anxious about the job interview.
- I'd be devastated if you left me.
- I'm afraid of failure.
- I'm shy because of my upbringing.

Mistake 2: We tend to mistakenly attribute our fulfilling, enjoyable experiences to something other than the principle of THOUGHT. But our fulfilling, enjoyable, desirable feelings are THOUGHT-generated; *they* only ever come from within.

Examples:

- I'll be successful once I get the promotion.
- I'm secure because I've got money in the bank.
- I'll have a sense of freedom once I quit my job.
- I'm confident and outgoing because of my upbringing.

Our feelings, states and emotions can't possibly come from anywhere other than THOUGHT, because our experience is mind-made. We live in an inside-out world, and all our experiences (the ones we like and the ones we don't) only ever come from within, 100% of the time. Period.

As you can see, these two mistakes are the same misunderstanding. The false assumption that we're experiencing something *other than* the principle of THOUGHT in the moment is a misunderstanding, the *cause* of the contaminated thinking that keeps us from clarity.

It often *seems* as though our felt experience of life is coming from something *other than* the products of THOUGHT, but it doesn't work that way. Why? Because THOUGHT is always creating a perceptual reality, and our THOUGHT-generated perceptual reality always looks *real* to us.

> *Contaminated thinking, arising from the outside-in misunderstanding, is the only thing that ever keeps us from clarity.*

Imagine a snow globe that's been vigorously shaken. The snow fills the entire globe, obscuring everything else. But the moment you set the snow globe down, the snow starts to settle, and the liquid clears. Contaminated thinking is like the snow in the snow-globe: plentiful and impenetrable, but with no meaningful substance.

> *Clarity is like the liquid in a snow globe. It's always there, behind the scenes, ready to start emerging the moment you wake up to the inside-out nature of reality, the realisation that you're living in the experience of the principle of* THOUGHT *taking form in the moment.*

It tends to seem like we're each living in our *circumstances* (a world of jobs, friends, beliefs, cars, family, houses, personalities, money, colleagues, accomplishments, etc.) but we're each living in a mind-made *experience*.

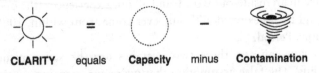

CLARITY equals **Capacity** minus **Contamination**

And that THOUGHT-generated perceptual reality is brought to life by the principles behind clarity. The principles behind clarity refer to the natural capacity for experience – thinking, feeling and perceiving – that we are born with. This innate capacity generates 100% of our experience of life, moment to moment.

Behind the Scenes

In 1974, a Scottish welder named Sydney Banks living in Western Canada had a sudden, transformational insight into the nature of experience. In a matter of moments he went from being a middle-aged man riddled with anxieties and insecurities to being calm, clear and peaceful, with a profound understanding of how our experience of reality is created.

The *Oxford English Dictionary* describes a principle as "the fundamental source or basis for something." As time passed, Banks started to talk in these terms, explaining that our experience of life is governed by principles. You can think of these principles as the source of (and basis for) 100% of our experience. These are the fundamental principles behind clarity.

THOUGHT: *The Reality Principle*
People think. The principle of THOUGHT refers to the innate capacity to generate a perceptual reality, an outer and inner world that we can see, hear, feel, taste and smell. This principle is also the source of the countless thoughts and perceptions that arise in the course of a day.

CONSCIOUSNESS: *The Experience Principle*
People are aware. The principle of CONSCIOUSNESS refers to our capacity to have an *experience* of THOUGHT taking form in the moment. CONSCIOUSNESS brings our THOUGHT-generated experiential reality to life and provides the sense of "I am-ness" we all share.

MIND: *The Power Principle*
People are alive. The principle of MIND is the "intelligent energy" that shows up in all aspects of the natural world. MIND is the power source behind life. Various cultures and fields have different names for this power: life force, universal energy, chi, nature, the great spirit, God, the no-thing, evolution, random chance and so on. You can think of it in whatever way makes sense to you.

These three formless principles are the "inside" I'm referring to when I say your experience is being created "from the inside out." The three principles are "inside"; everything else is "outside."

Inside	Outside
The formless principles of. . .	Everything else including. . .
• MIND • THOUGHT • CONSCIOUSNESS (your true identity)	• Time, space and matter • Personality/self-image/self-concept • Beliefs, thoughts and concepts • Physical bodies • Current circumstances • Past and future • Feelings and emotions

Once again, I'm not saying "you create your own reality"; I'm saying these principles are creating your unique *experience* of reality from within, moment to moment. We spend our lives moving through a dizzying variety of *experiential* realities, many of which bear little or no relation to any *objective* reality (if you doubt this, just cast your mind back to your last sexual fantasy).

So what's the point of learning about principles?

Principles are a source of massive leverage. When you understand the principles behind something, it increases your power, influence and impact exponentially. For example. . .

The principles of flight

People struggled for centuries to create flying machines. While people saw birds and insects flying, they didn't understand the principles that made flight possible. Then the Wright brothers discovered the *principles* of aeronautics. In December 1903 they achieved the first manned, machine-powered flight. In the century since, the world of aeronautics has achieved extraordinary feats (the helicopter, the jump jet, the space shuttle and the Concorde to name but a few). Discovering the principles of aeronautics gave people massive leverage to create things that couldn't even be dreamt of previously.

Reality Check

You may be saying, *"Hang on a second! Gravity is a principle, but you can measure gravity. How can you measure THOUGHT, CONSCIOUSNESS and MIND?"*

We *don't* actually measure gravity; we measure its effects. We know that if you drop a pencil, gravity will cause it to fall to the floor. By observing falling objects, we can draw conclusions about gravity, as Galileo and Newton did.

Similarly, you can't measure the principles behind clarity, but you can observe and measure their effects. In fact, as you continue deepening your understanding of these principles, you're going to start seeing the effects on a daily basis. Just as there are no exceptions to gravitation, there are no exceptions to these principles; they're a constant.

Our mental functioning influences every aspect of our lives on a daily basis. Understanding the principles behind the experience of life gives you massive leverage. The *implications* of these principles are profound for individuals, organisations and entire societies.

Another example: Even a *rudimentary* awareness of principles has implications for your behaviour. While you may only have a basic understanding of germ theory, it's likely that you've learned to wash your hands regularly, cover your mouth when you cough and are careful when handling anything you think is a significant source of bacteria.

Subtractive psychology is a user-friendly coding of the principles that govern our experience, and the implications of those principles. As you continue getting a deeper understanding of the principles behind clarity, you'll start experiencing a gentle yet powerful transformation, with more clarity, well-being and inner security. And why does insightful understanding of these principles make such an impact in people's lives?

Clarity of understanding leads to clarity of thought.

The outside-in misunderstanding – the mistaken belief that we're feeling something *other than* the principle of THOUGHT taking form in the moment – is the only thing that ever keeps us from clarity. The outside-in misunderstanding is a false assumption. Clear up the misunderstanding, and the mind clears.

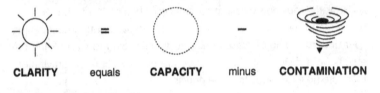

CLARITY equals **CAPACITY** minus **CONTAMINATION**

The factory settings

Clarity, inner security and well-being are the default setting for people; expressions of our true nature. They are our natural state when our minds are clear and free from contaminated thinking. As you continue deepening your understanding of the principles behind clarity, you'll start experiencing the "default settings" more of the time. These default settings are the "deep drivers" behind individual and business success.

Deep Driver	Description	What it drives...
Clarity: A clear mind, free from Contaminated thinking fully present and in the moment, with the levels of performance, satisfaction and enjoyment that brings.	The modern business world faces increasing complexity and rapid change while struggling with time scarcity, attention-poverty, information-saturation and communication overwhelm. Clarity is the ability to discern the factors that make a difference and act on them productively, without being distracted by the "noise" in the system.	<ul><li>High performance</li><li>Effective leadership</li><li>Presence</li><li>Insight</li><li>Confidence</li><li>Timely decision making</li><li>Detecting opportunities</li><li>Competitive advantage</li><li>Rapid response to change</li><li>Dealing with complexity</li><li>Productivity</li><li>Reduced stress</li><li>Increased focus</li></ul>
Direction: A sense of direction, purpose and motivation, free from urgency and undue pressure.	Every enterprise requires a clear sense of direction. A felt connection to a shared vision is a strong predictor of business success, yet it's surprising how often the people in a business have either lost sight of that shared vision, or no longer feel passionately connected to it.	<ul><li>Authentic leadership</li><li>Shared vision and purpose</li><li>Focus of resources</li><li>Employee engagement</li><li>Strategic planning</li><li>Brand clarity and passion</li><li>Sustainability</li><li>Resolves uncertainty</li><li>Shared goals</li><li>Motivation</li></ul>
Resilience: A strong sense of inner resilience, security and trust in yourself and your world.	Resilience is essential for dealing with the ups and downs of life. It's the deep driver behind why some people (and businesses) bounce back in the face of setbacks,	<ul><li>Thriving through uncertainty</li><li>Rapid recovery from setbacks</li><li>Dealing with change</li></ul>

Deep Driver	Description	What it drives. . .
	while others struggle to recover. Yet most people in business don't understand where resilience comes from, or how to cultivate it.	• Responsiveness and flexibility • Confident delivery • Agility and staying power • Mental fitness/toughness
Creativity: A reliable source of creativity and insight for innovating and solving problems.	Creativity is the driver behind all problem-solving and innovation. Consequently, it's an essential power-source for all businesses. Yet it's often overlooked, or seen as the domain of advertising agencies or other "creatives."	• Soft and hard innovation • Problem-solving • Disruptive strategy • Blue ocean strategy • Product and service design • Customer delight • Market leadership • Brand narrative • Opportunity creation
Connection: Warm, genuine connections with other people, leading to stronger relationships with clients, colleagues, friends, family-members and lovers.	Relationships in a business are a key measure of business strength. Strong relationships with customers result in loyalty. The benefits of strong colleague and supplier relationships are equally evident. Connection is the deep driver behind strong relationships.	• Understanding customer needs • Service culture • Employee engagement • Effective meetings • Productive, agile teams • Collaborative solutions • Contribution and caring • Sustainability • Social marketing • Effective communication • Effective listening • Persuasion and influence • Word of mouth/referrals • Brand loyalty

Deep Driver	Description	What it drives. . .
Authenticity: The freedom to be who you are, speak your truth and do what you believe to be right	The rise of social media has put businesses under increasing pressure to demonstrate transparency, integrity and authenticity. This trend is set to continue, and authenticity is the deep driver that will differentiate the companies that "walk the walk" from those who just "talk the talk."	• Authentic leadership • Integrity • Transparency • Customer loyalty • Employee engagement • Brand clarity and passion • Trust and credibility • Raving fans • Differentiation
Intuition: Alignment with your intuition and inner wisdom, your internal guidance system.	Whether you call it intuition, wisdom or "gut feel," business leaders from Richard Branson to Steve Jobs have acknowledged it as one of the key drivers in creating market-leading results. But few businesses understand what it is, how it works and how to develop it.	• Effective decision making • Opportunity spotting • Disruptive offerings • Blue ocean strategy • Market leadership • Soft and hard innovation • Product and service design • Competitive advantage • Sustainability
Presence: Present, aware and available to the moment, connected with your mind, your body and the world around you.	Presence is a rare quality, but when someone has it, other people sit up and take notice. Presence brings with it playful curiosity, charisma and enhanced awareness, making it a particularly attractive and sought-after quality.	• Influencing others • Charismatic leadership • Clear view of reality • Enhanced awareness • Enhanced forecasting • Trend-detection • Opportunity spotting • Natural attractiveness • Embodied learning

Expectation management

While these deep drivers are your birthright, nobody experiences them all the time. You're living in a THOUGHT-generated perceptual reality before you know THOUGHT has anything to do with it, so contaminated thinking comes with the territory. But you can look at it like the lanes on a motorway: the ability to notice and make adjustments when you're drifting out of your lane is far more important (and realistic) than trying to stay in the middle of your lane 100% of the time.

Breaking News!

I was once invited to *Sky TV's Breaking News* studio to be interviewed live, on-air, watched by over 5 million people (England's cricket captain was about to resign, and Sky wanted to get a psychological perspective on his decision-making).

It was to be my first time being interviewed on the TV news. As I waited offstage, I was feeling nervous (i.e. my head was full of contaminated, outside-in thinking). While I knew on one level that my feelings were coming from the principle of THOUGHT, they still looked and felt real to me.

Another guest noticed my anxiety and asked what I was going to do about it. My reply shocked him. *"Nothing,"* I said. *"I know that if I leave my thinking alone, I'll have what I need when I'm on air."* I explained that I didn't need to be in a "high-performance state" while I was offstage. When I was on air, I'd have what I needed to deliver the goods.

A production assistant came to collect me. My heart was pounding as I walked into the studio and took a seat across from newscaster, but as he introduced me, my head cleared. I put my attention on listening to his questions as deeply as I could and gave answers I'm still happy with today.

Context-sensitive

The mind is context-sensitive. The principles behind clarity point to an extraordinary "intelligence" capable of giving you what you need when you need it. The mindset that's most practical and useful for a job interview isn't necessarily the one that will give you the richest experience of sharing a sunset with your lover. The mindset that's most effective when coming up with a solution to a serious business problem isn't necessarily the one that will help you deliver the goods when you're delivering an inspirational speech to rally the troops.

Having all the resources to deal with the situation at hand is one of the *implications* of a deeper understanding of *subtractive psychology*. The more deeply you understand how the system works, the more you get to benefit from the implications of the principles behind it.

Even when we know about them, we all sometimes lose sight of the fact that principles are creating our experience of life. We get caught up in our thinking and slip into the outside-in illusion (the principles are creating that experience too!) Fortunately, there's a brilliant system we've each been given letting us know when that's happened, and pointing us back in the direction of our innate well-being.

Please allow me to introduce you to. . .

---

keep exploring ÷ connect with others
share your discoveries ÷ deepen your understanding

Thought Experiment: *I invite you to open to the possibility that the qualities people prize most highly (clarity, creativity, love, peace, presence and freedom, to name just a few) are traits you already possess. How surprised would you be if you were to suddenly realise these qualities are your natural state when there's nothing else in the way?*

What the Research Says: In his fascinating TED Talk "Do We See Reality As It Is?" cognitive neuroscientist Donald Hoffman uses a computer's desktop as a metaphor for perception. Just as 100% of your computer's desktop and the icons are generated from within the deeper properties of the device, 100% of the desktop and icons of your perception (i.e. space, time and the physical and nonphysical forms/objects you perceive) are generated from within the deeper properties of life. These deeper properties are by definition formless; they are what *generates* the forms of your perception (the desktop and icons). At the end of his talk, Hoffman says. . .

When I have a perceptual experience that I describe as a brain, or neurons, I am interacting with reality, but that reality is not a brain or neurons and is nothing like a brain or neurons. And that reality, whatever it is, is the real source of cause and effect in the world – not brains, not neurons. Brains and neurons have no causal powers. They cause none of our perceptual experiences, and none of our behavior.

Hoffman, D., Singh, M., & Prakash, C. (2015). The interface theory of perception. Psychonomic Bulletin & Review, 22, 1480–1506.

You can access the paper at www.JamieSmart.com/research/Clarity4

Additional Resources

www.JamieSmart.com/Clarity4

5

The Psychological Immune System

....

"The major problems in the world are the result of the difference between how nature works and the way people think."

Gregory Bateson
Epistemologist

"You're feeling your *thinking*, not what you're thinking about. . ."

My friend looked bemused by my statement. He'd asked me to cure his fear of flying, so I started by asking how he knew when to start becoming afraid, and how he knew when to stop. He told me that it usually started a week before his flight, and dissipated 20 or 30 minutes into the flight.

"I've got some great news for you," I told him. *"You're not afraid of flying!"*

"I'm not?" he asked in surprise.

"No," I replied. *"You have fearful thinking about flying."*

"Isn't that the same thing?" he responded, dubiously.

"No, it isn't the same thing," I said. *"You're feeling your thinking, not what you're thinking about. . ."*

People are notoriously bad at predicting their felt response to imagined scenarios. David is sure he'll fall apart if he gets made redundant, but it turns out to be one of the best things that's ever happened to him. Jennifer is convinced that her job is the source of all her woes, but when she gets a new one, her woes come along for the ride. Michael is excited about starting a business, sure he's going to love it, but he ends up struggling with stress and disillusionment. Jennifer has massive self-doubt but starts her new venture anyway. As she begins making progress, she blossoms and thrives.

And why are we so bad at these predictions?

Because we're having an experience of the principle of THOUGHT *in this moment*, not whatever we happen to be thinking *about*.

The brilliance of the body

Our bodies and minds have developed over millions of years to survive in a world full of threats and opportunities. People (as well as many other creatures) are born with a powerful immune system that protects them from disease and illness. The immune system reflects an innate tendency towards health and wellness that also shows up in the body's ability to repair wounds, breaks and other injuries.

We also have built-in systems to save our lives in the presence of danger. Fear is a powerful survival signal, an intense feeling of distress and alarm that can be used to alert us to a danger in our immediate environment and move us to take action: fight, flight or freeze. The purpose of fear is to keep us alive and to protect us from dangerous situations. If you're sitting in Starbucks and a hungry tiger saunters through the front door, fear can be a beautiful evolutionary gift that saves your life.

Whether you attribute these powers to a biological life force, to a creative intelligence, to the awesome engine of evolution, to random chance; whether you attribute them to all four or to none of the above, the fact remains: they're extraordinary abilities.

All of this happens without any conscious intervention; you don't have to think about it. In fact, most of the repair and regeneration your body has done in your lifetime has taken place without you even being aware of it. Your natural instinct to recoil from a hot flame or put your hands up to protect against a blow are expressions of the same deeper tendency towards health, wellness and survival. But there's something you may not have realised until now. . .

You also have a psychological immune system.

Just as we receive pain signals to let us know when our physical well-being is under threat, we also receive signals that wake us up when our heads are filling up with contaminated thinking.

The tip of the iceberg

The portion of an iceberg that's visible above the water's surface typically represents only 11% of the iceberg's total volume. Looking at the tip doesn't tell you anything about the shape of the submerged portion of the iceberg.

Our THOUGHT-generated perceptual reality is like an iceberg. . .

We live in a THOUGHT-generated experiential reality; 100% of our experience is created by the principle of THOUGHT taking form and being brought to life by CONSCIOUSNESS, moment to moment. But the individual thoughts that we notice going through our minds (i.e. what we're thinking *about*) are like the tip of the iceberg; they only comprise a tiny portion of our THOUGHT-generated experience in each moment. Like the submerged portion of the iceberg, the majority of our thinking is invisible.

So how do you know what's in the invisible portion of your thinking? Feelings. Feeling and thinking are like two sides of the same coin. Your felt experience is the "visible" face of the totality of your visible and invisible thinking.

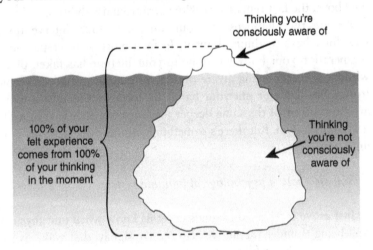

Figure 5.1 The Thinking/Feeling Iceberg

Reality Check

Some people object: *"Are you seriously trying to tell me that getting punched doesn't hurt unless you think it does?"*

No, I'm not saying that. But 100% of your *experience* of a punch (or anything else) comes to you via THOUGHT, the reality principle. You never feel anything that isn't being created via the power of THOUGHT. There are plenty of everyday examples of this fact:

- The scratch, bruise or cut that you don't discover until minutes or hours after it happens. It wasn't in your THOUGHT-generated experience when it happened, so you didn't feel it.
- The problem that you dwell on and worry about all day, then forget about entirely while watching a particularly engaging film that

evening. Something else is occupying your THOUGHT-generated reality, so you don't experience the problem.
- The lamppost you walk into as you're thinking about something else. The lamppost isn't in your THOUGHT-generated perceptual reality until you walk into it; then it *is* in it!

So what does this have to do with clarity?

When we believe we're feeling something *other than* THOUGHT in the moment, our minds fill up and speed up. The more contaminated thinking we have in any moment, the less clarity we experience. The less contaminated thinking we're in, the more clarity we experience.

Fearful thinking

I went on to explain to my friend that if flying were *genuinely* the cause of his anxiety, he would be at his *most* frightened when the plane was in the air, and it wouldn't start diminishing until after the plane had landed. The fact that he spent the major portion of the flight feeling fine meant that he wasn't afraid of flying; he was experiencing something else entirely.

International disasters such as the 9/11 World Trade Center attacks, the explosion of the space shuttle *Challenger*, and the BP Gulf oil rig disaster all have one thing in common: in every case, the official investigations reported that early warning signs were either ignored or misinterpreted. The fact is that, no matter how clear a signal is. . .

A signal is only as good as your understanding of it.

Thought Experiment

Imagine a malicious driving instructor who teaches a new driver that a green traffic light means "stop" and a red light means "go." If the learner driver ever tried to drive through a city, there would be chaos! The traffic signals would be working perfectly well, but the driver's misunderstanding of the signals would likely lead to a collision. While this example is as unlikely as it is are absurd, it raises two important points:

1. Misunderstanding of valid signals can lead to extreme difficulties.
2. All it takes to solve a misunderstanding is a realisation: insightful understanding.

How to Recover from a Tailspin

In the early days of aviation, a pilot's worst enemy was the tailspin. Planes would unexpectedly go into a rapid, spinning descent that typically ended in a fatal crash.

If a plane went into a spin, the pilot's impulse (based on their training and experience of flying under normal conditions) was to pull back on the stick, but this only served to make a tailspin worse. For years, it was common knowledge that if a pilot was unlucky enough to find themselves in a tailspin, they were doomed.

In 1912, Lieutenant Wilfred Parke went into an accidental tailspin at 700 feet while flying his biplane. Parke pulled back on the stick, but the plane continued its terrifying death plunge. Then, with only seconds to live, Parke did something utterly counterintuitive; he applied full right rudder. Onlookers watched in amazement as the doomed aircraft suddenly levelled out at 50 feet. Lieutenant Parke had just discovered how to get out of a tailspin!

"Parke's Technique" was revealed in 1912, but pilots continued to die because of their impulse to pull back on the stick if they went into a spin. They understood it intellectually, but they didn't have the insightful, embodied understanding that would save their lives. It wasn't until 1914, at the start of World War I, that pilots started receiving the training that would allow them to practise tailspin recovery. Experiencing it for themselves under controlled conditions gave them the insightful understanding that would save their lives if they ever went into an accidental tailspin.

The trick is not minding that it hurts

In a famous scene from the classic film *Lawrence of Arabia* (Horizon Pictures, 1962), T. E. Lawrence (played by Peter O'Toole) slowly extinguishes a burning match between his thumb and forefinger while his men look on in amazement. One of the men, William Potter, tries to replicate the feat, but recoils in pain. . .

Potter: "Ooh! It damn well hurts!"
Lawrence: "Certainly it hurts."
Potter: "Well, what's the trick then?"
Lawrence: "The trick, William Potter, is not minding that it hurts."

The pain withdrawal reflex is an involuntary response that moves your body (or part of your body) away from a source of pain. If you've ever accidentally touched a candle flame or a hot stove, you've experienced the pain withdrawal reflex. While the response is involuntary (i.e. not under your conscious control), it's still mediated by THOUGHT; a person who is under the influence of drink or drugs will not always exhibit the response, and people can actually be conditioned to override it (as Lawrence did).

The mental equivalent of the pain withdrawal reflex is most clearly exhibited in children under five years old. Toddlers can go from excruciating mental torment one minute to laughing and giggling the next. Even the most extreme tantrum doesn't last for long in the big scheme of things, certainly not as long as most adults' bouts of contaminated thinking.

A little child will only go so far into a painful thinking and only stay there so long before the "mental pain withdrawal reflex" kicks in and guides them back to clarity. The psychological immune system takes care of their mental well-being just as the physical immune system takes care of their physical well-being. So why isn't this response so obvious in teenagers and adults?

People can be conditioned to override it. . .

The natural system we have for guiding us out of painful preoccupations gets overridden by our conditioning. So if we've been conditioned to override it, how do we "wake up" when we're lost in thought?

That's where your psychological immune system comes in. Babies are born with a fully functioning psychological immune system – mentally ill infants are few and far between. But as they grow up, they get conditioned into thought habits of their family and their culture, thought habits that include the outside-in mis-understanding. Some people are less conditioned by it than others; you probably know some people who seem to be unusually resilient and philosophical in the face of hardship and crisis, just as you know others who seem to fall apart at the slightest provocation. The variable is this:

> *People who seem to fall apart at the slightest provocation are convinced their thinking is real. People who are resilient and resourceful in the face of hardship and crisis intuitively know their thinking is an illusion.*

So how do you begin to "see through" this conditioning? Realisation. Insightful understanding. As you continue reading this book and deepening your understanding of *subtractive psychology*, you'll start to notice stale habits of contaminated thinking dropping away and clarity emerging to take their place.

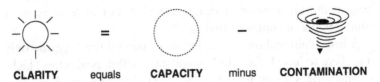

CLARITY   equals   **CAPACITY**   minus   **CONTAMINATION**

Rumble strips

On motorways, highways and autobahns all over the world, rumble strips along the edge of the road alert drivers who are travelling too near the edge. The signal is simple and well understood: they've started to go off-track. The moment a driver starts feeling the rumble, they correct their course easily.

We all drift off the road into contaminated thinking; it's part of our experience. But as you start to see through the outside-in misunderstanding, something changes. At some point when you start to go off track, it will occur to you that your feelings are coming from the principle of THOUGHT. This is the start of your psychological immune system's self-correcting process. You don't need to do anything to help it along; the process of self-correction is an automatic function of the mind.

And everyone has it!

In Chapter 8, I'm going to be introducing you to a new paradigm for how people learn, change and grow. Just knowing about its existence is going to have a huge impact for your increasing clarity. But first, some questions. . .

So if everyone has this powerful and elegant system built into them, why do so many people spend so much of their time riding on the rumble strips? If everyone's got this natural ability to find clarity and wisdom, why is there so much stress, pressure and conflict? So much crime, divorce, addiction and war? If everyone has an innate guidance system for keeping them on track, why does it so often seem like they're not using it?

For the answer to these questions, please let me introduce you to. . .

---

keep exploring ❖ connect with others
share your discoveries ❖ deepen your understanding

Thought Experiment: *"The major problems in the world are the result of the difference between how nature works and the way people think."* *Take a moment or two to reflect on Gregory Bateson's statement. By definition, it must apply to the problems of business, of relationships, of our personal struggles. Could it really be this simple?*

What the Research Says: In her paradigm-busting 1997 book, *Individual Differences in Post-traumatic Distress: Problems with the DSM-IV Model,* Professor Marilyn Bowman, PhD, conducted a meta-analysis of the available research on post-traumatic stress disorder (PTSD). She found that, while the field of psychology assumes a causal connection between "adverse events" and the experience of trauma, this is not borne out by the research. In the book's conclusion, she states the following:

The prevailing model used by clinical psychologists, psychiatrists and other mental health professionals predicts that toxic events will normally trigger clinically significant distress symptoms in a dose-response manner. This event-focused model is very poorly supported by the evidence. When prospective and representative samples are followed, most people do not respond to toxic events with serious and long-term distress disorders in the way that is assumed to be a normal, traumatic response in both professional and popular models.

Bowman's book goes into the topic in depth. You can find her article on the subject at the following link.

Bowman, M. (1999). Individual differences in post-traumatic distress: Problems with the DSM-IV model. *Canadian Journal of Psychiatry, 44*(1), 21–33.

You can access the paper at www.JamieSmart.com/research/Clarity5

Additional Resources

www.JamieSmart.com/Clarity5

6

Habitual Thought Patterns

··

"What the thinker thinks, the prover proves."

Leonard Orr
Writer and philosopher

"It took a long time for my thinking to get this messed up, so it's going to take a long time for it to get sorted out. . ."

Everyone nodded in agreement. It seemed to make sense. The phrase was one I'd heard countless times during my recovery from alcoholism, and its speakers had a positive intention: to acknowledge the (sometimes slow) learning and growing process of recovery, in contrast to the "instant fix" of drugs, alcohol and other substances.

But this simple piece of "received wisdom" also reveals a basic confusion people tend to have when it comes to the mind.

People tend to think, speak and act as though their thought forms have the same qualities as the material world.

Look at the following phrases:

- "The company's issues are really deep-rooted. They won't be easy to resolve."
- "This is a really big problem. It's going to be tough for our team to sort it out."
- "It took a long time for my thinking to get this messed up, so it's going to take a long time for it to get sorted out."

Each of these phrases has at least one example of the speaker attributing qualities from the material world to their thinking. (See table overleaf).

We all intuitively know that our thoughts are
fleeting and ephemeral.

That's why we write down phone numbers, notes and to-do lists; we recognise that if we don't write it down before we go to the shops, it may be gone when we next look for it. Yet we don't seem to remember that fact in other areas of our lives.

What the thinker thinks, the prover proves

Leonard Orr summed it up nicely when he explained that you can model the mind as having two key functions: a thinker and a prover. The thinker can believe absolutely anything:

- The world is flat/round/spherical.
- People are wonderful/nasty/only human.
- Life is hard/easy/a bowl of cherries.
- Change is a struggle/natural/effortless.

The thinker has infinite flexibility, but the prover has a much simpler job; what the thinker thinks, the prover proves:

- If you think this book is boring, you'll experience it as boring.
- If you think this book is fascinating, you'll experience it as fascinating.

Phrase	False Implication	Reality
"The company's issues are really deep-rooted. They won't be easy to resolve."	Issues have *roots*, and some *roots* are *deeper* than others. And of course, the *deeper* the *roots* are, the less easy the issues are to resolve.	Describing something as "an issue" is an act of perception, a thought. The idea that issues have roots is also a thought. The idea that that roots have depth and the deeper they are, the trickier that makes them to resolve is also a thought. All these thoughts are made of the principle of THOUGHT – a formless energy – so they're not subject to the laws of the material world. There are countless examples of "deep-rooted" issues that have been resolved quickly and easily. Especially when a person understands the nature of THOUGHT.
"This is a really big problem. It's going to be tough for our team to sort it out."	There are these things called *problems*, they come in different *sizes* (small, medium, large) and they need to be *sorted out*. The *bigger* they are, the more *difficult* they are to *sort out*.	When a person or group perceives something as a problem, it means they've got a way of perceiving a situation that they're labelling "problem." Whether large or small, it's all THOUGHT-generated. When a person has a realisation, their thinking (which may have looked like a big problem five minutes ago) is suddenly "sorted out," even though they didn't do anything to sort it out.
"It took a long time for my thinking to get this messed up, so it's going to take a long time for it to get sorted out."	*Messy thinking* is like a messy office or a garden that hasn't been cared for. The more *time* that elapses as it gets messy, the more *time* (and effort) it's going to take to *sort it out*. Like some enormous warehouse full of stuff, the more time spent on making it messy, the longer it takes to tidy it up.	THOUGHT is a creative energy, and the thought forms we create using it have no substance; they're literally made of "the stuff that dreams are made of." Have you ever noticed how fleeting dreams can be? How one minute you're experiencing a rich dreamscape, and the next minute you're wide awake and having trouble remembering what the dream was even about? The dream is so fleeting because it's made of THOUGHT. And your thinking is made of the same thing. It can change instantly the moment you have an insight. Time is a function of the material world, but THOUGHT isn't subject to the laws of the material world. People can experience a moment of clarity and see their lives change radically in a matter of moments.

Remember: THOUGHT is the best special effects department in the world, powered by MIND and brought to life in our experience by CONSCIOUSNESS. Our thinking always looks real. We're each living in a THOUGHT-generated experiential reality that *seems* like an actual reality, but it's not. And the moment we realise that, we step into a new world.

So if we each have innate clarity and resilience, and our thinking is just "the stuff that dreams are made of," why are so many people in thrall to their habitual thinking? Why are the plagues of stress, pressure, addiction, greed and hostility wreaking such havoc in the world? If little children demonstrate the characteristics of clarity – presence, joy, creativity, connection, resilience and so on – why is that so often NOT the case in older children, teenagers and adults?

There are several reasons. . .

- Little children intuitively know they don't really understand how life works. They haven't bought into a game plan for living, a set of rules that they have to try and fit themselves into.
- As a result, small children have comparatively little habitual thinking. Their experience of life is largely uncluttered by their cognitive models. The perceptual channels that allow a person to deeply experience the richness of life haven't been clogged up with habitual patterns of contaminated thinking.
- Consequently, little children haven't yet learned that there's anything wrong with thinking whatever they think, and feeling whatever they feel. They're not trying to correct their thinking or trying to change their feelings. When they feel angry, frightened or sad, they're fully committed to it, and when it's over, it's over. They feel whatever they feel, then allow themselves to return to clarity.
- Furthermore, they haven't bet the farm on their personal model of how life works. They know that they don't know. They intuitively get that their understanding of how life works is incomplete, provisional and subject to revision at any time.

- Plus they have an intuitive feel for the illusory and transitory nature of thoughts. They haven't been conditioned out of the psychological equivalent of the pain withdrawal response.

Of course, as children grow up, the self-correcting quality of their minds does get paved over by conditioning. They create habitual patterns of contaminated thinking and relate to those patterns as a reality.

Medication Time. . . Medication Time. . .

I started drinking alcohol when I was 12 years old. By the time I was 20, I was what's referred to as a "high-functioning alcoholic." I loved the feeling of peace, freedom and aliveness that alcohol gave me. But I was deeply troubled by the effects it had on my life, and the lives of those around me. I tried to control my drinking, but every attempt at control eventually resulted in greater chaos. By the time I was 30, I was done. I had a moment of clarity and decided to stop drinking. But things went from bad to worse. After 9 months without a drink, I was depressed and suicidal. My habitual patterns of contaminated thinking were robbing my life of any sense of peace, joy or aliveness. So I decided to get help.

Over the past 25 years, I've come to see the alcoholic's drinking, the drug addict's using, and every other addict's seemingly pathological behaviour as an example of medicating. And what is the addict trying to medicate?

Habitual patterns of contaminated thinking that seem like they're a material reality, like there's more to them than THOUGHT.

The addict's use of drink/drugs/sex/shopping/gambling is an "intervention" that offers temporary relief from contaminated thinking and the painful feelings that often accompany it. Similarly, many of the behavioural problems people experience are the result of an attempt to medicate agitated feelings that *seem* like they're coming from something *other than* THOUGHT taking form in the moment.

Remember: Many of the biggest disasters of the last few decades were the result of misinterpreted signals, valid signals that weren't properly understood.

Similarly, many of the behavioural problems people experience (ranging from distraction to addiction) are the result of an attempt to medicate agitated, uncomfortable feelings that seem like they're coming from something *other than* THOUGHT in the moment.

Contaminated thinking (and the feelings that accompany it) is all that ever stands between us and the high levels of clarity, security and peace of mind we all have within us.

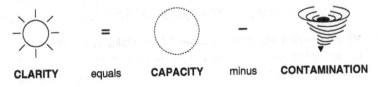

CLARITY   equals   **CAPACITY**   minus   **CONTAMINATION**

The river still flows

Imagine a river that starts to cool as winter comes. As the temperature falls, ice crystals begin to appear along the riverbanks. As it keeps getting colder, the ice crystals start forming small blocks of ice that break free of the banks and start flowing down the river. At various points the blocks of ice cluster together and the surface of the river starts to freeze over. Eventually, the surface of the river is a solid sheet of ice. But all the while, just beneath the surface, the river still flows.

Our habits of contaminated thinking are like the ice on the surface of the river: the only thing that ever stands in the way of clarity and a rich experience of life. But beneath that seemingly solid mass, the river still flows. Just as the ice was created from flowing water, our habits of contaminated thinking are created from THOUGHT, the formless energy behind our experience of life.

And behind all our contaminated thinking, the endless river of THOUGHT is still flowing, carrying the powerful gifts of our innate clarity, resilience and well-being to the surface of our aware-ness, bringing fresh new thinking to solve our problems and create new possibilities.

Sydney Banks often referred to the principle of THOUGHT as "the missing link," saying:

> *Thought is the missing link that gives us the power to recognize the illusionary separation between the spiritual world and the world of form.*

The illusionary separation? Yes. At the heart of all contaminated thinking is the false belief that we are separate from (and at the mercy of) a world "out there" in space and time, with power over how we feel. But that's an illusion. Who you *really* are can never be separated from the oneness of life. Here's how I put it in my book *RESULTS*:

> *Your experience flows from and is directly connected to* MIND, *the source of fresh, pure perception.*
>
> *When you fall out of contaminated thinking, even for a moment . . . that source of pure being starts refreshing your awareness, and clarity emerges.* THOUGHT *is the river that unites you with the world you perceive, and with the source of pure being.*

Of course, when we're locked in a mind-made prison of habitual thought, it seems ludicrous to think that freedom could be so near-by. At least, until you realise you've got the key. . .

keep exploring ⚹ connect with others
share your discoveries ⚹ deepen your understanding

Thought Experiment: *Is it possible that many of the things you've been experiencing as problems until now are a reflection of the mistaken belief that your thinking was real?*

What the Research Says: People often ask me what the difference is between thoughts, thinking and the principle of THOUGHT. A few years ago, I was answering a question from one of my Clarity Certification Training clients and came up with a metaphor to describe the principles behind clarity and how they create our perception (you can listen to that audio at the link below).

What I'm pointing to (metaphorically) in this audio is one of the most unexpected and counterintuitive facts about perception, first discovered in 1852 by Hermann Helmholtz. Here's an excerpt from the fascinating book, *Making Up The Mind: How the Brain Creates Our Mental World* by Chris Frith (Blackwell Publishing, ©Chris Frith 2007):

As a young research student, Hermann Helmholtz was told by his professor that it would be impossible to measure the speed of nerve conduction. It would be too fast. But, like all good students, he ignored this advice. In 1852 he was able to measure the speed of nerve conduction and showed that it was rather slow. In sensory neurons it takes about 20 msec for the nerve impulse to travel 1 meter. Helmholtz also measured "perception time" by asking people to press a button as soon as they felt a touch on various parts of the body. These reaction times turned out to be even longer, being more than 100 msec. These observations show that our perception of objects in the outside world is not immediate. Helmholtz realised that various processes must be occurring in the brain before a representation of an object in the outside world appears in the mind. He proposed that perception of the world was not direct, but depended on "unconscious inferences." In other words before we can perceive an object the brain has to infer what the object might be on the basis of the information reaching the senses.

This strange-but-true fact of our perception is utterly counter to how our perception of reality typically seems. Whenever I catch a glimpse of it, I'm struck afresh by how extraordinary this fact is. As such, it is worthy of reflection and wonder. I encourage you to listen to this brief audio (less than nine minutes) several times.

You can listen to the audio at www.JamieSmart.com/research/Clarity6

Additional Resources

www.JamieSmart.com/Clarity6

7

Stress: The Source and the Solution

....

"You're always living in the feeling of your thinking."

Keith Blevens, PhD
Clinical psychologist

"What are you looking for?"

The time was 2 a.m. The policeman had just walked round the corner to find an intoxicated-looking man on his hands and knees, searching frantically beneath a streetlight.

"I'm looking for my key," the man slurred.

"Where did you lose it?" the officer inquired.

"I dropped it in the long grass on a vacant lot, a couple of blocks away," said the man, still searching.

"Then why are you looking here?" asked the puzzled cop.

The man rolled his eyes and said, *"Because the light's better here."*

The man's mistake in this Sufi joke is so obvious as to be ridiculous, but there are times when we are all that drunken seeker. Each of us is searching under a streetlight for the key that isn't there when we're looking to "the outside" for the security/resilience/well-being/creativity/confidence/connection/fulfilment/success we desire.

Remember: We don't walk around in our *circumstances*; we walk around in our *experience*. Everything in our experience is created using THOUGHT, the reality principle. Our experience of the world out there is a THOUGHT-generated experiential reality. Your perception is an illusion, a practical and compelling one, but an illusion nevertheless.

The source of stress

So what does this have to do with stress? Here's what:

> *The true source of stress is the mistaken belief that we're
> feeling something other than the principle of
> THOUGHT taking form in the moment. . .
> . . . that we're at the mercy of something other
> than our moment-to-moment perceptions; a world
> "out there" in space or time with power
> over how we feel. . .*

THOUGHT is the formless energy that creates the form of our moment-to-moment experience. Just as sand can be used to make any kind of sandcastle or sand sculpture, THOUGHT can create any kind of perceptual form.

The following table shows how this works. For simplicity's sake, I've laid it out *sequentially over time*, but in reality it all happens *simultaneously* and *instantaneously*. THOUGHT creates an entire experiential reality in an instant; we're in it before we realise THOUGHT has anything to do with it.

In Chapter 4, we saw that misdirection is the initiation of a train of thought based on a false assumption. The moment we believe our felt experience is coming from something *other than* THOUGHT in the moment, we've accepted a false assumption and climbed aboard. This is the inevitable result of believing that thinking and feeling are separate; they're not. Thinking and feeling are *one* thing; two sides of the same coin. Which means. . .

We're never stressed out about what we believe we're stressed out about. . .

We're only ever stressed out because we believe we're feeling something other than THOUGHT *taking form in the moment. . .*

How Stress Works

When we mistakenly believe our agitated, unpleasant feelings are coming from "out there," from something *other than* THOUGHT taking form in the moment (e.g. money, other people, the past, the future, health, what we're like, etc.). . .
↓
We automatically assume there's a world "out there" with power over our felt experience. . .
↓
Implying that we are separate from and at the mercy of that world "out there". . .
↓
And it seems vitally important to either get control of or escape from that world "out there" in order to secure/protect our well-being, now and in the future. . .
↓
And our heads fill up with contaminated thinking as we try to manage, manipulate and control that world "out there". . .
↓
Resulting in a congested, speedy mind. . .
insecurity, neediness, and isolation. . .
stress, worry and anxiety. . .
and so on

The belief that we're feeling something other than THOUGHT makes us believe we are victims. Some people respond to that by retreating, defending or manipulating, while others come out fighting; either way, they're responding to an illusion. Of course, this doesn't just apply to stress; everything from worry and anxiety to anger and rage can be the result of this subtle but catastrophic misdirection.

And, strange as it may seem, it can also apply to pleasant experiences. The idea that our fun/happy/enjoyable/exciting/loving feelings are coming from something other than THOUGHT in the moment is equally misguided; it just doesn't work that way.

Reality Check

Some people worry that life would be flat, dull and boring if they were to realise their felt experience is always coming from THOUGHT, but nothing could be further from the truth.

Once a person has a realisation about the nature of films, they're able to enjoy films *more*. We can still engage deeply with a film, being touched and moved, even though we understand how films work. The fact that we know our security isn't at risk allows us to enter *more* deeply into the experience.

In the same way, as you continue learning about the principles behind clarity, you'll find yourself entering *even more* deeply into the experience of life.

We're always and only feeling the formless principle of THOUGHT taking form in the moment. Period. It only works one way.

Even when it we believe we're feeling something other than THOUGHT, it still only works one way. . .

As mentioned previously, the principles behind clarity (THOUGHT, MIND and CONSCIOUSNESS) are *formless*. Before we delve into the "solution" to stress, it's worth exploring what *formless* means.

DISTINCTION: Form versus Formless

The THOUGHT-generated reality we each experience contains the **form** of life: the sights, sounds, smells, tastes and feelings that make up our inner and outer worlds. As tangible as it may seem, our experience of the form of life is actually a mind-made illusion (brought to you by THOUGHT, the best special effects department there is).

The *power* of THOUGHT, however, is **formless** by its very nature. Being formless, it can take any form. You can think of it as the *ability* to create a perceptual form.

The intellect is like a filing system for organising and manipulating forms. But the intellect is utterly incapable of "grasping" something formless. Example: Imagine a formless energy. What does it look like? Most people give answers like "a beam of light," "lightning," or "a cloud," but these are all forms.

When we describe something as "formless," we're effectively saying that it is in the domain of that which cannot be perceived by a human nervous system and its extensions (telescopes, microscopes, mass spectrometers, etc.). If you prefer, you can describe it like this:

MIND, THOUGHT and CONSCIOUSNESS are *spiritual principles*.

DISTINCTION: Tangible versus Real

When you watch a movie online (or one you've downloaded), something remarkable happens: The digital information encoded in the file is translated into a set of instructions that are relayed to the device you're using, and a dance of electrons appears on the screen. As you look at the screen, you transform that dance of electrons into an experience involving characters, plotline and action.

And it happens so fast, you don't even realise you're doing it. . .

We don't realise that we're experiencing an illusion as though it were a reality. We don't realise that we're breathing life into the dance of electrons and creating the relationships between the TV characters. The images on the screen are not **real**; they're an illusion that we bring to life with our minds. They're **tangible**, but not real.

Compared to the images on the screen, the information encoded in the file or data stream is relatively intangible. You can't tell much about the movie by looking at the data – it's just a collection of digits and symbols. But the data is giving *rise* to the images on the screen. In that sense, it's *more* real than the images on the screen. After all, the data can be used to play the movie on millions of screens simultaneously.

The *form* of life is a tangible illusion: tangible, but not real. The *formless spiritual principles* that create our experience are real, but not tangible. Our experience of life is in the form, but the power behind life is in the formless.

The light's better here

We innocently look in the tangible (but illusory) world of form for our clarity, well-being, security and success because the light's so much better here. But you can never find something where it isn't, no matter how hard you look. Our experience of the world of form is an illusion, an often-practical one, but an illusion nevertheless.

Your felt experience doesn't come from the illusion. . .

Your felt experience comes from what's creating the illusion. . .

It comes from the principles that are generating 100% of your experience of reality. . .

Because the intellect is a form-manipulation system and cannot conceive of something "formless"; we need to use metaphors to point to it. The words THOUGHT, CONSCIOUSNESS and MIND are themselves metaphors that point to the formless energy creating our experience of life.

As we go through life, we experience the form of our inner and outer worlds. The formless principles behind clarity are what's *creating* that experience.

So what does this have to do with stress? And with clarity?

Road Rage

The only thing that ever stands in the way of clarity is contaminated thinking: the false belief that we live in an outside-in world. Here's an example of how we might teach someone how to "do" contaminated thinking:

A survey of Britons conducted by Gillette found that people listed work, job interviews and traffic as the top three causes of stress. So let's imagine someone who has "stressful work" that they plan to quit and is stuck in traffic on the way to the job interview for a position they want (we'll call our job applicant Jeremy). For some reason, Jeremy doesn't know how to feel stressed about traffic, so we decide to teach him.

First, we tell Jeremy to think about the traffic and to start making mental forms (or objects) representing what traffic means to him: the causes and the consequences. We tell Jeremy to think about arriving late for the job interview and to imagine being stuck in his current job forever. We tell him to imagine that the other road users are deliberately trying to sabotage him and that vengeful engineers have rigged the traffic lights against him. Most important, we tell him to imagine that his security, happiness and well-being is at the mercy of these external factors. If Jeremy follows our instructions, his head should fill up with contaminated thinking, and he should start feeling tense, anxious and ill at ease. Finally, we tell him to imagine that the traffic is "causing" those feelings. Voila! We've just taught him how to have "traffic stress" (if he's *really* good at it, he might even be able to do road rage).

We're always experiencing the products of Thought in the moment. . .
But when we believe we're experiencing something other
than Thought it seems like we're feeling the things we're
thinking about.

It's not that the job interview doesn't matter or that the traffic isn't inconvenient; the issue is that when we're lost in contaminated thinking, we're not nearly as awake to our resilience, resourcefulness and creativity as we could be. Sitting in a traffic jam with *clarity*, Jeremy might think to change his route or call ahead and reschedule the interview. With clarity, he might even have found himself leaving early and avoiding the traffic in the *first* place.

The solution to stress

When we're lost in contaminated thinking, we tend to be obsessed with the "forms" of life. But, as clarity emerges, the forms don't appear to be important in the same way. Athletes often report that when they're in the zone, it seems as though, on the one hand, it doesn't matter whether they win or lose and, on the other hand, they're going to give it all they've got.

This doesn't even make *sense* as an intellectual construct, but as clarity emerges, it becomes self-evident. We naturally tend to be less concerned with the form of our thinking and more aligned with the principles creating it – a direction that's accompanied by a deeper felt experience of life and a sense of well-being.

While we don't all have the words to describe it, every one of us has experienced it. For one person it may be when they're walking through the woods or looking out at the waves on the ocean; for another person it may be when they're deeply involved in an activity like dancing or running. Sometimes, these moments of deeper connection find us "out of the blue." But they all share something in common. . .

When we have clarity and peace of mind, it's not personal. We don't tend to be caught up in the form of our contaminated, "it's all about me" thinking. Situations that may have seemed infuriating are suddenly no longer an issue. We "just know" things will turn out alright.

This deeper, more connected sense is a signal that you're looking away from the *form* of your experience and are more aligned with what's creating it: the formless principles of THOUGHT,

Consciousness and Mind. An understanding of the formless can be seen in a variety of domains, and goes by many names:

- The no-thing (Buddhism)
- The implicate order (Bohmian physics)
- The Tao (Taoism)
- Life energy (some biologists)
- Spirit (spirituality)
- God (many religions)
- The great spirit (North American Indians)

Many names, but one direction: looking beyond our experience of the form of life to where that experience is coming from.

So what's the "solution" to stress? A deeper insightful understanding of the inside-out nature of life. The moment we insightfully see that 100% of our feeling is coming from Thought in the moment (and not from anything *other than* that), feelings of stress start diminishing and clarity starts emerging. This doesn't make us immune to stress – we still get hoodwinked by contaminated thinking from time to time. But as you continue exploring the principles behind clarity, you'll begin to notice your stress levels decreasing in general and that you have a very different response to many things which used to stress you out.

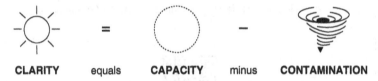

CLARITY equals **CAPACITY** minus **CONTAMINATION**

And why is insightful understanding likely to succeed in a world where the prevailing psychological paradigm identifies an increasing number of different mental disorders every year? Where governments throw their hands up in despair at the rise in addictions, depression and stress? Where businesses are paralysed in the face of disruptive competitors and increasing complexity? Where individuals battle with attention poverty, time scarcity and information overload?

The answer to all these questions is to be found in a newly discovered leverage point for transformation. . .

---

keep exploring ⟐ connect with others
share your discoveries ⟐ deepen your understanding

Thought Experiment: *What would it mean to you (and for you) if you were to suddenly realise that 100% of your felt experience is coming from THOUGHT taking form in the moment? That 0% of your feeling is coming from anywhere other than THOUGHT?*

What the Research Says: The only reference to the Gillette-sponsored stress research is a 2010 article in *Metro News*. As you read the article (via the link below), you'll see how the reporter's biases reveal themselves (e.g. "Moving house is obviously one of those distressing times, which brings on a lot of anxiety, so it's no surprise it came in fourth place, followed by exam time for students.") The presumption that distress is being "caused" by moving house is so "obvious" to the reporter that it doesn't even get questioned or examined. As you continue to deepen your understanding of subtractive psychology, you'll find these kinds of examples jumping out at you more and more frequently.

Metro Reporter. (2010). Top causes of stress revealed. *Metro News*.

You can access the article at www.JamieSmart.com/research/Clarity7

Additional Resources

www.JamieSmart.com/Clarity7

8

The Ultimate Leverage Point

....

"The historian of science may be tempted to exclaim that when paradigms change, the world itself changes with them."

Thomas Kuhn
Physicist, historian and philosopher of science

"Pay no attention to that man behind the curtain. Go – before I lose my temper! The Great and Powerful Oz has spoken. . ."

When I was a little boy, I loved the film *The Wizard of Oz*, but I was frightened of the Wicked Witch of the West and terrified of her flying monkeys. I would hide behind the sofa when they came on the screen. On some level, I didn't understand that those monkeys were just people in costumes, and that even if they really *were* flying monkeys, they couldn't escape from the television screen.

I didn't understand the nature of film.

And I'm not alone. In 1896, the Lumiere brothers showed a motion picture in public for the first time in history. The film was a 90-second clip of a train arriving at a station, and showed the train moving towards the camera. The audience were excited to be part of this "cinematic first," but when the film started playing, many of them ran screaming from their seats.

They didn't understand the nature of film.

They didn't realise there was no way the train could escape from the screen and plunge into the audience. They saw patterns of light moving on a screen and responded to a THOUGHT-generated illusion as though it was a material reality.

Hallucinations

One of my first ever coaching clients had a dog phobia. I asked her *"How do you know when to get frightened?"* Her head shot back, and she said *"As soon as I see the gnashing jaws,"* while using her hands to mimic a dog snapping at her face. When she saw a dog, even if it was 50 feet away and on a lead, she would generate this frightening hallucination and respond accordingly.

She was responding to a THOUGHT-generated illusion as though it was a material reality.

It's easy to laugh at the Lumiere brothers' audience, or to dismiss my dog-phobic client's fear as "irrational," but each of us gets hypnotised by the same order of illusion on a daily basis. Whether a person is worrying or daydreaming, stressing out because they're stuck in traffic or getting excited about a date they're going on later, they're experiencing a THOUGHT-generated perceptual reality.

So what has this got to do with clarity?

Increasing clarity is the inevitable result
of a transformation in your understanding
of how your experience is being created and of
who you really are. . .

Level 1: Material reality

The material world is bound by certain laws, such as gravity. If a person drops a brick on their foot, it will likely do some damage. If a person exercises regularly, their muscles will get stronger.

Level 2: The content of thinking (what you're thinking about)

Sigmund Freud popularised the idea that the content of a person's memories "caused" their current experience. Making changes at this level is like changing the content of a movie (or making up stories about the impact of movies you watched in the past).

Level 3: The structure of thinking

The originators of neuro-linguistic programming (NLP) came to the conclusion that the *structure* of a person's thinking plays a significant role in shaping their experience. Making changes at the level of structure is like playing with the shot selection, camera angles and soundtrack in a film.

Level 4: The nature of THOUGHT

Sydney Banks realised in a profound way that THOUGHT creates our multisensory "picture" of reality; our experience of the world is created from the inside out via the principles of MIND, THOUGHT and CONSCIOUSNESS. Insightfully understanding what's *behind* the scenes of our experience (i.e. seeing the nature of THOUGHT) can lead to a profound transformation, increasing clarity, security and peace of mind. People often experience a significant reduction in stress and an increase in their sense of resiliency, regardless of external circumstances. Longstanding problems and issues often disappear without being "worked on."

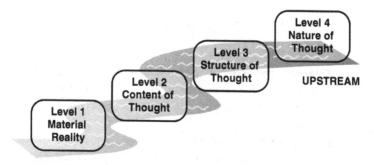

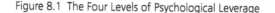

Figure 8.1 The Four Levels of Psychological Leverage

When it comes to film, the most powerful shift a person can experience is a shift in understanding. Once a person insightfully understands the nature of films, they can watch movies that would previously have put them in fear for their lives.

Until a person understands the nature of film, it can really seem like those flying monkeys are going to come out of the screen and get them. But they won't. Ever. Because that's not the nature of film. It doesn't work that way.

Until a person understands the nature of film, the best they can do is keep reminding themselves that "It's just a movie, it's just a movie. . ." Once a person insightfully understands the nature of film, they don't need to do *anything*. No further intervention is necessary. They can still be deeply affected by a movie, but they know their well-being isn't at risk.

> *Until a person understands the nature of* THOUGHT, *intervention at the level of content or structure seems to make sense. Once you insightfully understand the nature of* THOUGHT, *intervention at the level of content or structure loses its appeal.*

The flying monkeys can't get out of the TV. The train's never getting out of the screen. Ever. . .

DISTINCTION: Externally Corrected versus Self-correcting

- **Externally corrected:** A system that needs an external agent to diagnose problems, then take action to put them right, can be referred to as externally corrected. If a car breaks down, it won't fix itself.
- **Self-correcting:** A self-correcting system requires no external intervention; it just needs the right conditions and enough time

> to resolve any issues. The primary condition required for a self-correcting system to find its way back to balance is simple: an absence of external interference.

Subtractive psychology is grounded in implication-based learning. It focuses on helping a client to insightfully understand the nature of THOUGHT and the principles behind how our experience is created. As such, there is no need for external correction.

Like understanding the nature of film, as soon as a person gets an insight into the nature of THOUGHT, their entire experience of reality starts to change. They start living in the implications of that understanding. Certified Clarity Coaches, Consultants and Practitioners work with clients to help them get an insight into the nature of THOUGHT, secure in the knowledge that the client really does have everything they need to self-correct, to find clarity, solve their problems and create the results that matter to them.

The Power of Understanding

I once, collected my daughters from the home of a relative who was suffering from conjunctivitis (an extremely unpleasant and contagious infection of the eye membranes). I was careful not to touch anything, because I had a workshop to deliver, followed by a flight to California (my colleague Cathy Casey and I were due to share this understanding with inmates in the gang unit of San Jose Maximum Security Jail, work that Cathy had been pioneering for over a decade.) The last thing I needed was a trip to the doctor.

Later, I ate a hot, spicy meal, then sat down to watch a film with my children. That's when my eyes started itching. Over the course of the next 20 minutes, my eyes became more and more irritated, and my heart sank. I had conjunctivitis! My head filled with visions of doctors' waiting rooms, eye drops and cosmetic unpleasantness. When my misery reached epic proportions, I announced that I was going to take a shower.

> The warm water had been running over my face and neck for about 90 seconds when a small, quiet voice inside me said "you got chili sauce in your eyes." In less than a second, my anxiety levels evaporated as my spirits rose like a helium balloon. The physical symptoms were just as unpleasant, but there was a key difference; I knew that the cause of my problem was a minor inconvenience (chili sauce) not a serious problem (an eye infection).
>
> In an instant, I popped from one reality into another, and my world changed.

There's a huge difference between intervening in an existing perceptual reality versus looking upstream at what's creating that perceptual reality. If a person doesn't understand that they're feeling the principle of THOUGHT taking form in the moment, they'll accept what their perception has to tell them about those feelings.

THOUGHT creates the world then says "I didn't do it. . ."

However, the moment a person starts to insightfully understand the nature of THOUGHT, they experience a freedom in relation to the experiential reality it's generating. This represents a new paradigm for our understanding of the mind.

The Power of a Paradigm

The term *paradigm* was coined by Thomas Kuhn in his groundbreaking book, *The Structure of Scientific Revolutions* (listed by the *Times Literary Supplement* as one of "The Hundred Most Influential Books Since the Second World War"). The *Oxford English Dictionary* describes a paradigm (in the Kuhnian sense) as "a worldview underlying the theories and methodology of a particular scientific subject."

Kuhn explains that every scientific field has a pre-paradigm phase, during which the field has no shared basis or foundation to build upon.

During this time, the field is beset by anomalies, with scientists working hard to explain them. Then, at a certain point, a paradigm emerges. Now the field has a shared foundation, a basis for further experiment and exploration. A new paradigm often results from the discovery of principles. For instance, Newton's discovery of the principle of gravity (and his resulting law of universal gravitation) established a new paradigm for physics, a foundation on which subsequent work was based. Einstein's work on relativity established a further paradigm. Schrodinger's and Bohr's work on quantum physics established yet another, and so on.

The field of psychology has been in its pre-paradigm phase until now. This explains the plethora of (often conflicting) theories, techniques and models. It goes some way to accounting for the "replication crisis" in psychology, whereby many psychology experiments have proved impossible to reproduce. It also explains the many thousands of books published each year on personal development, business psychology and leadership models.

What Sydney Banks' discovery of the principles underlying experience makes possible is the realisation of a single paradigm: a worldview underpinning the theories and methodologies of all aspects of psychology.

When we shift from the pre-paradigm phase to the acceptance of a single paradigm, it has a profound impact. Consider these examples in the table overleaf.

Once a paradigm is established, it renders many pre-paradigm theories obsolete. The flat-earth theory, the geo-centric universe and the miasma model are now seen as quaint historical curiosities. The principled, single-paradigm model of psychology (summarised in the statement "we're living in the experience of the principle of THOUGHT taking form in the moment") puts numerous other psychological models and theories to rest.

Contaminated thinking (the mistaken belief that we're experiencing something *other than* THOUGHT in the moment) is bogus, a groundless illusion, as obsolete as the flat-earth theory, the geo-centric universe and the miasma model.

Field	Pre-paradigm	Post-paradigm
Solar system	Believed planet Earth was the centre of universe. Calendars were inaccurate. Had to make occasional calendar adjustments to catch up. Difficulty predicting movement of planets and so on.	Saw that the sun is the centre of the solar system. Calendars were made more accurate. Greater ability to predict movement of planets and so on.
Germ theory	Believed disease and illness were caused by a range of factors including miasmas and atmospheres. Doctors innocently made matters worse. Disease spread and exacerbated due to misunderstanding.	Near-universal awareness of germ theory. Individuals take sensible precautions to avoid illness. Doctors and nurses scrub up. Massive reduction in illness, and near eradication of many diseases. Significantly increased average life span.
Flight	Countless attempts to create a manned, powered aircraft, using a variety of ingenious methods, with not a single successful flight.	The Wright brothers' discovery of the principles of aeronautics lead to manned aircraft, international jet travel, the emergence of package holidays and so on.

The pioneering psychologist William James stated that if fundamental principles governing psychology were ever discovered, it would be the most important discovery for humanity since we mastered fire. The principles William James dreamt of have been discovered. Insightful understanding of this new paradigm is growing even as you read this book.

I've seen profound transformations in my clients as they get an understanding of the nature of THOUGHT. People start making progress on dreams that had seemed impossible until now. Business teams start working together and delivering results more creatively and effectively than ever before. Conflicts get resolved, and relationships get back on track. Clarity increases and performance improves. People suddenly discover that they've got more time in the day (a result of spending less and less time in contaminated thinking). Individuals often start experiencing a quality of life and peace of mind unlike anything they've experienced until now.

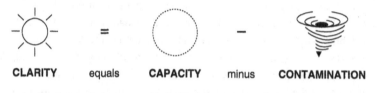

CLARITY   equals   CAPACITY   minus   CONTAMINATION

And what's the source of the kind of clarity, creativity, presence, authenticity, motivation, connection, resilience, peace of mind and enjoyment of life most people yearn for?

I'll give you a hint: You've already got it. . .

keep exploring ÷ connect with others
share your discoveries ÷ deepen your understanding

Thought Experiment: *One of the more profound implications of the principles behind clarity is this: You don't need to control, monitor or manage your thinking. What happens when you stop for a moment and deeply consider that?*

What the Research Says: In his classic book, *The Structure of Scientific Revolutions*, Thomas Kuhn mentions a piece of research conducted by Bruner and Postman, "On the Perception of Incongruity: A Paradigm" (1254 citations).

In their experiment, the researchers presented a mix of standard and doctored playing cards to participants (for example, the 3 of hearts – a red suit – might be doctored to be the colour black). They discovered that until a certain threshold was reached, participants would identify the doctored playing cards according to the standard patterns they were more familiar with. Once a threshold was reached, participants would exhibit a variety of "threshold reactions" including confusion and cognitive distortions (e.g. one of Bruner and Postman's subjects exclaimed, "I can't make the suit out, whatever it is. It didn't even look like a card that time. I don't know what color it is now or whether it's a spade or a heart. I'm not even sure now what a spade looks like. My God!")

The paper's conclusion states that

Perceptual organization is powerfully determined by expectations built upon past commerce with the environment. When such expectations are violated by the environment, the perceiver's behavior can be described as resistance to the recognition of the unexpected or incongruous. The resistance manifests itself in subtle and complex but nevertheless distinguishable perceptual responses. Among the perceptual processes which implement this resistance are (1) the dominance of one principle of organization which prevents the appearance of incongruity and (2) a form of "partial assimilation to expectancy" which we have called compromise.

This is what Kuhn was so struck by. When we have a set of expectations about how some aspect of reality is, we tend to organise new information to fit with those expectations.

Bruner, J., Postman, L. (1949) On the Perception of Incongruity: A Paradigm. First published in *Journal of Personality*, 18, 206–223.

You can access the paper at www.JamieSmart.com/research/Clarity8

Additional Resources

www.JamieSmart.com/Clarity8

PART TWO

The Deep Drivers

9

Innate Clarity and Peace of Mind

....

"We don't know who discovered water, but we know it wasn't the fish."

Marshall McLuhan
Media theorist

"I don't need you to change. And I don't need anything from you. Whether you believe it or not, you don't need to do a thing..."

I burst into tears.

The year was 2004, and I'd just travelled several hundred miles to have a session with a coach. When I arrived, I explained that I really wanted to make some changes, and that I was totally committed to doing whatever I needed to do to get the most from our time together. I said that I felt like I really needed a breakthrough, and I was worried that if I didn't "get it right," my time and money would be wasted, and I would be no further forward. Worse still, I would be stuck in the stress, disease and hopelessness that had me come to him in the first place.

He told me I didn't need to do anything, and I burst into tears. And as I sat there with tears streaming down my face, I started to feel more peaceful.

We sat and talked for three hours, and by the time we were finished, I felt better than I had in ages. And I was so happy that I was feeling better, I didn't think to ask some obvious questions. . .

1. Where do the deep, rich, profound feelings in life come from?
2. Where do they go when you're not aware of them?
3. What are the factors determining whether you're aware of them or not?

Your understanding of how life works

Your understanding of how life works and who you really are has more influence than *any other factor* over your experience of life and the results you get. We each behave in accordance with what makes sense to us:

- In Aztec culture, it "made sense" to sacrifice people to the gods in order to keep the community thriving.
- In England in the 1850s, it "made sense" to dump raw sewage into the River Thames and carry small bunches of flowers to protect against illness.
- In Japanese culture, it "makes sense" for many people to work 12 hours a day, 6 days a week, for months or even years on end, with an inevitable toll on their health and well-being (the Japanese even have a word, *karōshi*, which means literally "death from overwork").

In 2004, my understanding of "how life works" dictated that all feelings and states could be re-created, accessed and utilised by manipulating a person's body, their breathing, and their thought patterns. Mental-emotional states were something a person "chose," "got into" and "managed." I endeavoured to direct, alter and manage my thought patterns in order to experience the states, feelings and emotions I wanted.

I saw states, feelings and emotions as a result. They were something I "did." If I wasn't feeling the way I wanted to feel, it just meant that I wasn't choosing, getting into or managing the states well enough.

In the cultures of NLP, CBT and positive psychology, it "makes sense" to focus on directing, managing and controlling your thinking in order to experience the states you believe will serve you.

But, as you start to understand the principles behind clarity more deeply, the idea of managing your states in this way shows a misunderstanding of what states, feelings and emotions are; the idea of "state control" stops making sense.

You have innate clarity and peace of mind

Clarity and peace of mind are the default position for people – the factory settings. While these are context-sensitive – they can show up differently depending on the situation – they're the baseline for a person when there's nothing else in the way. And what gets in the way? Contaminated thinking.

Like a football being held underwater, as soon as you let go, it rises to the surface. And like the grass pressing up through the cracks in a city pavement, resilience and clarity are always doing their best to find their way through the paving slabs of contaminated thinking. . .

If you have any doubt about this, consider little children. Up to the age of about four years old, children return easily to the default setting of clarity and well-being. While they often get upset, they don't stay with it. The pull of clarity is too strong, and their contaminated thinking is not powerful enough to keep them from it. The average three-year-old:

- Tends to be deeply engaged, easily amused and satisfied with the simple joys of life; is present and in the moment
- Doesn't know the meaning of the word *bored*; can enjoy the same things over and over again

- Is loving and open-hearted, connecting easily with others
- Finds lots of things fun and funny
- Comes up with new ideas and creative insights
- Knows they don't really understand how life works; is curious, often puzzled, and constantly learning
- Gets over upsets quickly and easily; doesn't tend to dwell on past mistakes or worry about the future
- Is in touch with their deeper wisdom, often aware of "the elusive obvious" that the adults around them aren't seeing

The average three-year-old spends a lot of their time in clarity, because they're allowing their psychology to do what it's *developed* to do. Ironically, the extremes of emotion that little children swing back and forth between would look *certifiable* if shown by the average adult, but that's because children aren't trying to manage their states. The psychology of little children is an example of the mind's self-correcting system given the freedom to do what it does best: return to a set point of clarity and well-being.

Think of a child's gyroscope. When the gyroscope spins, it naturally gravitates towards a vertical alignment. If you knock it off centre, it self-corrects and makes its way back towards the vertical. You don't need to do anything to correct it – in fact, efforts to correct it tend to *impede* its progress.

The mind is a self-correcting system.
Its set-point is clarity, resilience and well-being. . .

Case Study: Dragon's Den

My client and close friend Rich Enion was in a bind. He had just appeared on TV's *Dragon's Den* seeking funding for *BassToneSlap*, a business providing drumming-based performances, teambuilding and experiential marketing events. Dragons Peter Jones and Theo Paphitis had just offered him and his business partner £50,000 for a 40% share in the company. The offer had sounded good on the programme, but when it came time to sign contracts, Rich was having second thoughts.

While he was tempted by the prospect of a healthy cash injection, the thought of surrendering a big chunk of his business and profits was daunting. He was stuck in a dilemma and didn't know what to do.

Rich asked my advice, so I talked to him about the nature of THOUGHT, the reality principle. I explained that his feelings of doubt and confusion weren't coming from the deal, the money, the percentages or the potential results; they were coming from the power of THOUGHT in this very moment. As we continued exploring, Rich got quiet. After a few moments of silent reflection, he took a deep breath and said he had the answer. I asked him what had occurred to him, and he said *"Freedom!"*

Rich explained that the appearance on *Dragon's Den* had been the result of an authentic desire and many months of hard work and focus. He'd intuitively known what an incredible opportunity it was. The offer of investment seemed like the icing on the cake, but somewhere along the way, Rich had lost sight of why he and his partner created *BassToneSlap* in the first place. . . Freedom! From Rich's perspective, the purpose of the business was so they could create great experiences for clients while doing something they loved, with plenty of space in the diary for travel and adventure.

When Rich got clear and reconnected with the purpose for the business, he realised that signing the contract with the Dragons would be a wrong turn. They declined the £50,000, and stayed connected with the vision. *BassToneSlap* has grown into a successful business; Rich has a number of teams that he joins for performances when he's in the UK. The rest of the time, he runs his business from exotic locations around the world, enjoying the freedom he's found.

And it turns out that the cumulative benefits of allowing the self-correcting mind to find its way back to clarity and peace of mind vastly outweigh the tactical benefits of external intervention. Why? Because external intervention interferes with the self-correcting system doing its job.

Remember: THOUGHT is the best special-effects department in the world. Your THOUGHT-generated perceptual reality always seems real. You're always and only feeling the principle of THOUGHT taking form in the moment, but it often seems as though you're feeling something other than THOUGHT.

Clarity is what a person's psychology is always endeavouring to return to. Innate clarity and resilience are always shining a beacon, even when a person seems extremely lost.

Modello, Homestead Gardens and Coliseum Gardens

In the mid-1980s, Dr Roger Mills introduced "Health Realisation" (a community-oriented presentation of the inside-out understanding) to residents of Modello and Homestead Gardens, two Florida housing projects that had become havens for drug dealers, and hotbeds of addiction, crime and abuse.

At first, the residents were suspicious of this man trying to point them towards the clarity and well-being he claimed was already within them. They (understandably) saw their horrific circumstances and backgrounds as the source of their problems. But slowly, people began to catch on, and get a feel for the direction Dr Mills was pointing them towards.

By the time the programme completed two years later, the community had seen a greater than 50% improvement in employment levels, school attendance and parent/school involvement. The drug dealers had gone, and there was a massive decrease in criminal activity.

Residents had found their innate clarity and peace of mind.

The experiment was repeated in Oakland's Coliseum and Lockwood Gardens. The homicide rate in these housing projects went from being the highest in the city to zero – a level they remained at for the next ten years. In addition to the zero homicide rate, violent crimes dropped by 45%. Police officer Jerry Williams received the California Peace Prize in 1997 for his leadership of the initiative.

Innate clarity, well-being and resilience exist within every person; it's your natural state, something you become particularly aware of when you've got nothing on your mind. In fact, there's nothing you need to do to have an awareness of innate clarity and peace of mind; it's more of a not-doing. You see. . .

Clarity isn't an achievement;
it's a pre-existing condition.

It's not something you need to practise or work on; it's an expression of who you really are.

The infinite creative intelligence of MIND shows up in every aspect of our experience, gently pointing us towards clarity and well-being. The capacity for clarity is there within each one of us, tirelessly working to guide us in the direction of our most inspiring, rewarding and meaningfully successful lives.

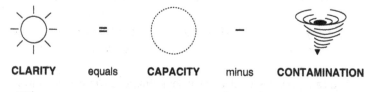

CLARITY equals **CAPACITY** minus **CONTAMINATION**

When you turn your attention away from the grinding familiarity of contaminated thinking, you make space for clarity and the powerful inevitability of fresh, new thought. That's when you find yourself looking in the most generative, nourishing and resourceful direction there is. . .

---

keep exploring ❖ connect with others
share your discoveries ❖ deepen your understanding

Thought Experiment: *What happens when you open to the possibility that clarity, resilience and peace of mind are your default settings?*

What the Research Says: In his 2021 book, *Thriving in the Eye of the Hurricane*, author and principles teacher Joe Bailey describes training programmes he and Dr Keith Blevens created and delivered for the world-renowned Mayo Clinic in Arizona. These programmes were designed to address burnout in physicians, and they showed impressive results. The programmes were based on the principles we're exploring in

---

this book. (Blevens and Bailey are pioneers in the understanding of these principles.) Participant surveys showed the following:

- 64% ruminate less about challenges in their work
- 75% report they rebound more quickly from adversity
- 78% said the course was helpful in reducing stress and burnout
- 79% are less emotionally reactive to other people and circumstances
- 92% said they would recommend the course to others

Participants reported "improved effectiveness, efficiency and perspective, which facilitate better relationships with coworkers. They also find more ease in difficult conversations, better decision-making which leads to better teamwork, and improved work/life balance."

Bailey, J. (2021). *Thriving in the eye of the hurricane: Unlocking resilience in turbulent times (find your inner strength)*. Mango.

You can access the book at www.JamieSmart.com/research/Clarity9

Additional Resources

www.JamieSmart.com/Clarity9

10

Creativity and Disruptive Innovation

....

"You don't learn to walk by following rules.
You learn by doing, and by falling over."

Richard Branson
Entrepreneur, founder of Virgin Group

"It just occurred to me when I was out for a walk in the woods. . ."

In 2003, I started a business creating educational products. Each week, I wrote an article and sent it to my subscribers. By the end of the first year, after 5000 people had subscribed to my articles, I had a sudden insight. Google had recently launched Adwords – little adverts that showed up when you searched the web. I could run ads for my newsletter and pay a low price for each new subscriber. It was years before anyone else caught on.

By 2008, I had one of the largest email lists in the industry, with more than 80,000 subscribers in my tribe. I explained my Adwords "secret" to a marketing expert who was interviewing me, and he asked me where I got the idea. "I don't know," I said, "It just occurred to me when I was out for a walk in the woods."

Now I know where that innovative new idea came from; it came from the unknown...

DISTINCTION: The Known versus the Unknown

The known is the database of *thoughts* you've already had, including your beliefs, concepts, ideas; your habitual ways of thinking about yourself, your life and your world. By definition, the thoughts you've already had are rooted in the past; while they can hold valuable information, they're yesterday's news and can only tell you about what *was*.

The unknown is the source of all fresh, new thoughts, the formless power of THOUGHT. When we have clarity, our minds are free from contaminated thinking, and we create space for new insights and realisations to flow in. (All your "known" thoughts originally came from the unknown, too, back when they were fresh, new and relevant.)

When people are looking for solutions, they tend to look to what they already know, but all too often the answers we need can't be found there. When we want fresh new ideas, creativity, solutions and changes, it pays to look to the unknown.

Looking to the database of the known for navigating the future is like looking in the rearview mirror to find your way forward...

Disruptive innovation

The pace of change is accelerating, and our world is getting more complex. *Disruptive innovation* is the phrase to describe when agile startups steal market share from major players or even take the market in a new direction. One of the surprising things about this is how often the major players peer into the database of the known, stuck in "analysis paralysis" as a new entrant gobbles up their market.

The music industry was like a rabbit in the headlights in 1999 when Napster enabled millions of users to share their music collections with each other. The record companies responded by clinging to a model designed for a world that no longer existed. They looked to the known for the answer, and they came up empty-handed; their revenues dropped by 50% between 2001 and 2010. Meanwhile, Apple launched the iTunes store in 2003, making it possible for customers to purchase and download music online *legally*. Apple threw a life preserver to the music business, and they gave their customers what they really wanted, becoming the world's most profitable company in the process.

The gap

Epistemologist Gregory Bateson said that problems result from the difference between how nature works and the way people think. If we try to navigate using an out-of-date map, we run into problems; our thinking is out of step with reality. But the music industry (and many other businesses) clung to the map of their habitual thinking in the face of overwhelming evidence that it was no longer fit for purpose. Why?

Fear. Insecurity. Lack of clarity.

The only explanation for this bizarre behaviour is that they were lost in contaminated thinking, hypnotised by the outside-in misunderstanding, unable to see clearly. Contaminated thinking can make it seem as though the unknown is dangerous, and the database of habitual thinking is a safe refuge, but nothing could be further from the truth.

So what's the alternative? Insightful understanding.

> *Realisations close the gap between how you*
> *believe life works and how life really works...*

What Showers and Vacations Have in Common

Senior executives were surveyed and asked where and when they tended to get their best ideas. The top three answers were as follows:

1. On vacation
2. In the shower
3. While travelling to and from work

The ideas that really made a difference arrived at the very times that they *weren't* thinking about work, in situations where they weren't looking for answers in what they already knew.

Almost everyone can relate to this and find their own examples of a fresh, new thought arriving when the mind is in a more relaxed, contemplative state. Yet, all too often, when people want to find an answer, solution or fresh new idea, they grind away at what they already know, running through their habitual thinking patterns one more time.

Ironically, the habitual thinking they're grinding away at is typically the only thing standing between a person and a fresh new idea. Habitual thinking is "the box" that corporate facilitators are chronically telling us we need to "think outside" of.

Throughout history, many of the most profound and groundbreaking new ideas did not come from the reorganisation of what people already knew; they came from the unknown, in the form of insights, realisations and sudden "a-ha" moments:

- The Greek mathematician, physicist and inventor Archimedes had been grappling with the problem of how to determine the volume of a golden crown that King Hiero II suspected of being impure. One day, as he climbed into his bath, Archimedes saw the water level rise, and had a sudden realisation about how he could solve the problem. He shouted "Eureka" and ran naked into the street. He'd been working fruitlessly within what he already knew as he'd tried to figure out the problem, but his realisation came from a realisation, a fresh new perspective. It came from the unknown.

- By 1666, Isaac Newton had already been struggling for some time to describe the workings of gravity. One day, sitting in his mother's garden in "a contemplative mood," he happened to see an apple fall from a tree. Suddenly, he had an insight about the nature of gravity. Newton's theory of gravitation grew from this fresh, new thought, a realisation that came from beyond what he already knew, from the unknown.

- In 1920, Otto Loewi (the father of neuroscience) was fast asleep when he had a dream in which he envisaged an experiment that could prove conclusively how nerve impulses were transmitted. Scientists had been theorising about it for 15 years, but Loewi's realisation took the field from theory to fact. Loewi's fresh idea came from the unknown.

Of course, the unknown isn't just available to scientists and mathematicians. We all have a source of fresh new perception, beyond what we already know. . .

- The insight that gives you the elegant solution for something that had you stumped
- The realisation that has you understand something that used to baffle you
- The "a-ha" moment that gives you a fresh new perspective on a situation.

Whether you call it an insight, a realisation, or an "a-ha" moment, new arrivals from the unknown almost always come with a feeling of peace and clarity, a gentle rightness and "knowing" that feels fresh and new.

 = −

CLARITY   equals   **CAPACITY**   minus   **CONTAMINATION**

So if the unknown is such a rich and powerful resource, why are so many people "afraid of the unknown," building elaborate structures of stale, contaminated thinking as a vain attempt to protect them against what they don't yet know?

Every vertebrate instinctively knows that in the *material* world, the unknown can be an unpredictable place of potential risks and rewards, while the known may have a proven track record of safety, security and predictability.

But we make a mistake when we attribute the same qualities to the world of our thinking.

The known of our thinking is often like an out-of-date map that doesn't show any recent developments: the new streets, parks and paths of possibility. We can search the map as much as we like, but we won't find something wonderful that's just around the corner (or right there in front of us) if the map doesn't mention it.

So if it's off the map, where can you find it? And how can you benefit from the clarity, resilience and peace of mind that it brings?

---

keep exploring ✢ connect with others
share your discoveries ✢ deepen your understanding

Thought Experiment: *Just like there's no way to "un-stale" a loaf of bread, there's no way to freshen thinking that's past its use-by date. Fortunately, the principles behind clarity are like the baker's oven. They're always ready to produce fresh realisations as soon as it occurs to you that you won't find the answer in what you already know.*

What the Research Says: Author and cognitive scientist Dr Scott Barry Kaufman contributed to research into the relationship between showers and creativity. The consumer survey (commissioned by shower manufacturer Hansgrohe SE) interviewed 4000 people in countries around the world and found the following:

- 72% of people have experienced new ideas in the shower.
- 14% take showers for the sole purpose of generating creative thoughts and insights.
- More young people showered specifically for new ideas, fresh thinking or problem-solving.

Dr Kaufman goes on to speculate on some of cognitive science's explanations for *why* showers may have this effect.

Hansgrohe study: The brightest ideas begin in the shower. (2015, January 26). *Plumbing & Mechanical.*

You can access the article at www.JamieSmart.com/research/Clarity10

Additional Resources

www.JamieSmart.com/Clarity10

11

Authenticity: Your True Identity

....

"Matter flows from place to place and momentarily comes together to be you. Whatever you are, therefore, you are not the stuff of which you are made."

Richard Dawkins
Evolutionary biologist

"You are not your job. You are not how much money you have in the bank. . ."

These two "un-firmations" echo through *Fight Club* like an incantation. Fincher's classic film (and the Chuck Palahniuk book it is based on) raises questions about meaning, identity and the consumerist dream. In the process, it strips away the false identities of many of the characters through a mixture of fighting, fellowship and harrowing ordeals. And while the film continues to detail "who you aren't" (you are not the shoes that you wear, the contents of your wallet, etc.), it's less specific about who you *are*. . .

A Case of Mistaken Identity

Stop for a moment and touch your nose. Say the words, "This is my nose."

I've invited countless members of my audiences, workshops and teambuilding sessions to perform this simple task over the years. Everyone finds it easy to do, yet few of us consider the extraordinary accomplishments that make this possible.

When you were born, you didn't realise you had a nose, eyes and a face. Your hands and fingers were mysterious objects that emitted sensations and occasionally bumped into your head. You had no sense of them being "yours" or of your being able to control them.

But then something amazing happened. . .

You started to create a map; a map of *you*. It started with your body, your immediate environment and your parents. This map let you define the relationships between different parts of your body – essential for being able to perform actions like touching your nose or grasping an object.

You also created a map of "who you are," a map that you've been updating ever since. This map of "who you are" is sometimes referred to as the self-image, self-concept or ego. But please be clear: When I say you created a map, the "you" I'm referring to isn't that self-image, self-concept or ego.

The self-image gets used as a reference point for living, giving you an opinion on what you're capable of, where your limits are, what you deserve, what's important and so on. Whether you believe something's possible for you or not, it's likely that you automatically check with your self-image to find out its opinion, one way or another.

But here's the thing: Your self-image is a THOUGHT-generated map/model. It's not who you *really* are. Who you *really* are is the one that created it.

And while none of us would ever make the mistake of confusing a map of New York City with the city itself, we all make this same mistake when we confuse our self-image with our true identity.

You see, just as a *map* of New York is not New York, your *ideas* about you are not you. We each fall into the trap of believing our ideas about ourselves describe the entirety of who we are, but it's a case of mistaken identity.

You are not a label.
You are not your beliefs, thoughts or feelings
about yourself.
You are not the contents or structure of your thinking.
And who you really are is far, far more than you think. . .

Not only are you not your job, your bank balance or the shoes you wear. . .

- You are not your body.
- You are not your accomplishments.
- You are not your history.
- You are not your prospects.
- You are not your ideas about yourself.
- You are not your theories about what is or isn't possible for you.
- You are not your personality, self-image, self-concept or ego.
- In fact, you aren't the contents or structure of your thinking at all.

Think about it: If "who you really are" was your body, your self-image, or how you feel about yourself, then these things would never change; they would be constant. But that's not the case:

- **Your body:** Your body changes as you grow, age and develop. If you look at a picture of yourself from ten years ago, there are almost certainly differences. Our bodies are made mostly from water, and all the cells are frequently replaced. In fact, most of the cells in your body are less than ten years old! Who a person truly is doesn't change, but their body does. You call it "my body," but who is the "me" whose body it is?

- **Your self-image:** How you relate to yourself changes as you learn and grow and as you go in and out of contaminated thinking. One day a person comes home from work feeling bad about themselves. The next day they wake up feeling great about themselves. Your *true identity* doesn't change, but how you *perceive* yourself does. You call your thinking "my thinking," but who is the one who's having the experience?

- **Your feelings:** Your feelings change on a daily basis; you're living in the experience of the principle of THOUGHT taking form in each moment. You refer to your feelings as "my feelings," but who is the one who's feeling them? You refer to yourself as "me," but who is the one who is having an experience of being you?

Even trying to answer these questions can take you into a curious state, because they point in the direction of what I'm calling the formless. So if all of this is who you *aren't*, who *are* you?

Who you *really* are is what's *creating* your experience: the intelligent, formless energy behind life I'm describing as the principles of THOUGHT, CONSCIOUSNESS and MIND.

It's odd to think of who we really are as "energy," but it also stands to reason. Science tells us that everything is made of energy, that the atoms that make up our bodies are mostly space. The law of conservation of energy (a principle of the first law of thermodynamics) states:

Energy can be neither created nor destroyed. However, energy can change forms, and energy can flow from one place to another.

Biologist Richard Dawkins suggests that we are more like waves than things. He explains that all the atoms that were in our bodies as children have been replaced, that whatever we may be, we're not the "stuff" of our physical bodies. Different cultures and traditions through the ages have had a variety of ways of describing what we are and where we come from:

- Consciousness, soul, essence
- Big mind, the great spirit, God
- Natural intelligence, divine energy, the oneness

Each of these words are metaphors, pointing to something formless, intangible and constant, a "true identity" that sits behind the fleeting but tangible illusion of our material reality.

So how is this relevant?

Spiritual Capacity and Performance

In their *Harvard Business Review* article, "The Making of a Corporate Athlete," Jim Loehr and Tony Schwartz explain that, in addition to their physical, mental and emotional capacity, the most successful senior executives and entrepreneurs also attend to their "spiritual capacity," which they define as follows:

By spiritual capacity, we simply mean the energy that is unleashed by tapping into one's deepest values and defining a strong sense of purpose. This capacity, we have found, serves as sustenance in the face of adversity and as a powerful source of motivation, focus, determination, and resilience.

As you'll appreciate, the terms *deepest values* and *sense of purpose* are simply metaphors, forms that point to something deeper. Words like *team spirit* and *inspiration* are other examples of an attempt to point to something that comes *before* the world of form.

Who you *really* are – your essence – is the formless energy behind life, the principles behind clarity. The principles of THOUGHT,

CONSCIOUSNESS and MIND are also the source of your security, well-being, peace, joy and happiness, which means. . .

You already are *what you've been searching for until now.* . .

There's nothing to search for – you've already got it; you already *are* it. There's nowhere to get to – you're already here. . .

You don't need improving, fixing or developing – who you already *are* is the all-encompassing energy behind life!

Stop for a moment and consider the planet we live on. As you're reading these words, the energy behind life is moving from formless into form, and back again:

- Babies are being born.
- Flowers are blooming.
- Forest fires are burning.
- Birds are flying.
- Billions of people are breathing in and out (including everyone you know).
- Leaves are drifting to the ground and fallen branches are disintegrating.
- The heart of every mammal on the planet is beating.
- Water is evaporating.
- Subatomic particles are moving in and out of existence.
- Countless billions of thoughts are emerging then disappearing.
- Rain is falling.
- And on, and on, and on . . . all of this as you're reading these words. . .

Behind all of this is the energy behind life. It shows up in all the processes of your body and all the workings of your mind.

It's what's creating your perceptual reality, and it's what's experiencing the reality it's creating.

To paraphrase Cobb (the lead character from *Inception*) once again. . .

In your waking experience of reality, the principles behind clarity continuously create and perceive a world simultaneously. . .

So completely that you don't even feel them doing the creating.

So, if who we really are is this extraordinary intelligence – the formless energy behind life – why do we so often look, feel and act as though we're neither intelligent nor extraordinary? You guessed it: contaminated thinking and the outside-in misunderstanding that gives rise to it.

It's entirely natural and understandable that we get fooled by our thinking. But we can each wake up to a greater clarity of understanding in any moment.

The War of the Worlds

On Halloween night 1938, Orson Welles directed the radio version of H. G. Wells's novel, *The War of the Worlds*. It was a radio play with a difference; Welles presented it in the form of a news broadcast, giving a "live report" of New Jersey being invaded by Martians. He made it as realistic as possible, even getting the actors to study newsreels of the Hindenburg disaster so they could replicate the panic and terror in the voices of the announcers.

As far as numerous listeners were concerned, they had tuned in to a live news report. They reacted with shock and terror as they heard descriptions of tentacled Martians using heat rays to incinerate their fellow Americans. There was widespread panic, and some people even armed themselves and took to the streets.

They were responding to a THOUGHT-generated illusion as though it was a material reality.

The police were swamped with calls from terrified listeners. They told them all the same thing:

"It's just a radio show."

While a few callers may not have believed the police at first, we can imagine how most of them responded. . .

> Waves of relief. . .
> Relief, peace and even laughter are natural responses, the moment you realise you've been responding to a mind-made illusion, not a material reality. The moment they saw that it was a radio show and not a news report, their "problem" was solved.
> And how much effort did it take them to see the truth? None.

No matter how deeply asleep we are, we're only ever one realisation away from waking up. No matter how lost you sometimes get in dreams of lack, worry and insecurity, who you really are is always the same. . .

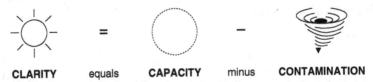

CLARITY   equals   **CAPACITY**   minus   **CONTAMINATION**

Peace, freedom, wisdom, clarity and love. You are what you've been searching for. Resilience, creativity, security, confidence and joy. You already are the source of all you desire, the energy behind life.

And just as a wave is not separate from the ocean, who you really are is not separate from the energy of the universe. . .

By the way, I don't mean energy in a woo-woo, New Age sense. I mean it in a more down-to-earth, scientific, "*this is the logical extension of what leading physicists are telling us*," sense.

So how can you align yourself with how the world *already works*? Fortunately, you've been provided with an elegant, accurate and reliable tool for navigating life, deepening your understanding, guiding you back to clarity and having a richer experience than you may have ever thought possible. . .

keep exploring ✣ connect with others
share your discoveries ✣ deepen your understanding

Thought Experiment: *What happens when you consider the fact that clarity, peace and security are only ever one thought away?*

What the Research Says: A 1978 research paper, "Development of Self-Recognition in the Infant" describes a variety of experiments to map the stages at which infants develop a sense of self.

One of the most memorable of these is the "rouge test." An infant is playing in front of a mirror, then a spot of rouge is discretely applied to the child's face. Before the age of 18 months, the infant does not recognise their reflection. They will even look behind the mirror to see if they can find that "other child." Then, from 18 months on, when the child catches sight of their image in the mirror, they react and touch the spot of rouge on their face (there are various YouTube videos of this experiment being done if you'd like to see it for yourself).

Sydney Banks often described the ego as "an image of self-importance." That "image" is the idea that "who we are" is that person in the mirror, effectively a third-person perspective on ourselves. The author Douglas Harding brilliantly explores this strange notion in his 1961 book, *On Having No Head*.

Bertenthal, B. I., & Fischer, K. W. (1978). Development of self-recognition in the infant. *Developmental Psychology, 14*(1), 44–50.

You can access the paper at www.JamieSmart.com/research/Clarity11

Additional Resources

www.JamieSmart.com/Clarity11

12

Intuition: Navigating by Wisdom

....

"Don't let the noise of others' opinions drown out your own inner voice. And, most important, have the courage to follow your heart and intuition. They somehow already know what you truly want to become. Everything else is secondary."

Steve Jobs
Entrepreneur, co-founder of Apple

"All that the pathfinder needs is his senses and knowledge of how to interpret nature's signs. . ."

In his book *Nature Is Your Guide: How to Find Your Way on Land and Sea*, record-breaking navigator Harold Gatty claims there is no such thing as a sense of direction. He explains that a person who *appears* to have such a "sense" is actually using their five *ordinary* senses (seeing, hearing, smelling, tasting and feeling), informing and informed by their experience and intelligence.

Gatty was a pioneer in the early years of aviation navigation. Before the existence of autopilot and other modern navigation technologies, Gatty mastered the art of using minimal cues from the natural world to orient the crafts he guided around the world; setting a direction, making adjustments and staying on track.

Today we have GPS satellite navigation and numerous other technologies, yet we still rely on our senses for much of our day-to-day orientation. Whether we're walking down a city street, moving around our living space or driving to a friend's house, we're supported in our journeys by our five senses, our intelligence and our experience.

But we make a mistake when we try to use exactly the same navigation system to make our way on the journey of life. Consider these statements:

- "I want to get clarity on my overall life path before I take the next step."
- "I'm stuck. My life's at a roadblock, and I need to get moving."
- "I need to define my values and purpose so I can start heading in the right direction."

Remember: People tend to think, speak and act as though their thought forms have the same qualities as the material world.

We use material world metaphors for our work, for our lives, for our problems. We create those metaphors and bring them to life using the principles of THOUGHT, CONSCIOUSNESS and MIND, then we respond to them as though they're a material reality. We conceptualise life as a journey, a struggle, or an adventure, then we start behaving as though that's actually the case!

When it comes to making our way through life, it seems as though the navigation systems that work in the material world should also work in the world of our life metaphors. For example: If life's a journey, then it stands to reason that you need to get clear on the destination, find a good map and ensure you take the right steps. If life's a game, then it looks as though you need to find out how to play, learn what the rules are and do your best to win. If life's a battle, then it makes sense to focus on weapons, strategy and tactics.

But life is not a journey, a game or a battle. Life isn't a bed of roses, a bowl of cherries or a box of chocolates. Life isn't a struggle, a lesson or even an adventure. . .

Life just is.

So if life "just is," how can we live a life we love? If we go beyond the comforting familiarity of our material world metaphors, how do we know where to go, what to do or what we even want?

The bad news is that metaphors are inherent in our language; any verbal answer to the previous questions will be strewn with them. The good news is that it doesn't matter. You see. . .

Fortunately, you have a built-in guidance system;
it's called wisdom. . .

Wisdom is an expression of MIND: the power principle. As such, it comes from before the world of form, from outside of our perceptual domain of time, space and matter. While intellect and past experience can be a valuable source of data, wisdom provides a different calibre of information. It's a context-sensitive, up-to-the-minute guidance system that comes from *before* your habitual thinking from the intelligent energy behind life.

When you're watching a film, the information in the file or data stream exists prior to (and gives rise to) the forms on the screen; similarly the source of wisdom exists prior to our THOUGHT-generated experiential reality.

Sat-nav for Your Life

Habitual, contaminated thinking is like an out-of-date map, a distorted snapshot of the world taken at the time it was created. It may have its uses, but the fact that you've already *thought* it means it's out of date. Wisdom, on the other hand, is like a constantly updated super sat-nav system for your life. Wisdom comes from *before* your habitual thinking, so it's never out of date.

Even a map you made as recently as last week can't possibly respond to road closures and traffic jams, but a high-quality sat-nav can.

And where is the sat-nav of your wisdom navigating you to? It's helping you find your way back home to who you really are, so you can have a richer, deeper, more fulfilling experience of life . . . so you can enjoy the high performance and good decisions that come from a clear mind . . . so you can create what you're inspired to create . . . so you can benefit from the innovation, resilience and clarity you need to prosper in times of uncertainty, complexity and change.

This innate wisdom is distinct from intellect and experience, so it's not dependent on any of the factors that are often cited as being associated with wisdom. It's unconnected with education, background, intellect, age and experience (little children, for example, sometimes exhibit a deep wisdom and intelligence about life despite their early years).

Why?

Because all of these "factors" are based in the world of form. But you can think of this innate wisdom as an "emanation" from the formless energy behind life. Everyone has the wisdom of the universe within them. No one has access to more wisdom than anyone else.

Who's on your "top three wisest people ever" list?

- Buddha, Christ, Muhammad?
- Socrates, Plato and Aristotle?
- Queen Elizabeth I, Abraham Lincoln, the Dalai Lama?
- Galileo, Isaac Newton, Marie Curie?
- Anne Frank, Ayn Rand, John Lennon?
- Albert Einstein, Stephen Hawking, Jane Goodall?
- Richard Branson, Anita Roddick, Steve Jobs?
- Mohandas Gandhi, Rosa Parks, Nelson Mandela?

Whoever's on your list, none of them has/had access to more wisdom than you. You have the same wisdom at the heart of your being as the wisest people in history. So, how do you become more and more open to that wisdom and allow it to guide you?

It's *already* guiding you, moment to moment. . .

In *Nature Is Your Guide*, Gatty makes the point that we use our sense organs instinctively. We don't have to be *taught* to use them; you didn't have to go to classes on how to see, hear, feel, taste or smell. The ability to use the senses arrives bundled with the senses themselves. Your ability to use your senses is innate. Some people are more attuned to certain senses than others, but we're all expressing an innate ability.

It's the same with wisdom. . .

- When you're feeling more and more agitated as you think about something someone did last week . . . that's wisdom, activating the "psychological pain-withdrawal reflex."
- When you're lost in contaminated thinking, and it suddenly occurs to you that you're experiencing THOUGHT in this moment . . . that's wisdom, pointing you back in the right direction.
- When you finally stop ruminating on a problem and the answer suddenly arrives . . . that's wisdom, penetrating the veneer of habitual thinking.
- When you're soaking in the tub and a flash of insight lets you know exactly how to proceed in an area where you were blocked . . . that's wisdom, giving you strategic guidance.

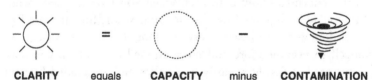

CLARITY　equals　**CAPACITY**　minus　**CONTAMINATION**

As you're probably already starting to intuit, "wisdom" is a way of referring to the day-to-day guidance that arises from your innate capacity for realisation.

The wisdom that comes with clarity is often accompanied by a good feeling, a sense of peaceful knowing and freshness that's very distinct from the "fervent rightness" of our habitual thinking. Bear in mind that wisdom is looking out for your best interests. And while that doesn't mean that everyone's going to *like* what you do when you act on wisdom, they'll often be able to "see the wisdom" in it. Wisdom often seems obvious in retrospect; people say things like "I don't understand how I didn't see it before." It's also worth remembering that wisdom is a kind of flavour of realisation and that you've already been acting on it in a variety of ways throughout your life.

Strategic Intuition

William Duggan is a Senior Lecturer in Business for Columbia University's MBA courses. In his award-winning book, *Strategic Intuition*, he explains that the flashes of insight that are so often the source of brilliant strategy almost never happen when people are thinking about the matter at hand.

Instead, they come when we're in the shower, or driving, or on holiday, when we're in a more reflective state, allowing our minds to wander.

So, if the solution to our most pressing problems is to be found in reflection and relaxation, why are we so tempted to chew away at them like a dog with a bone?

Contaminated thinking.

When we're caught up in the outside-in misunderstanding, the feelings that accompany what we're thinking about can make it feel like grinding away at it is a good idea, but that's a misinterpretation of a valid signal (see Chapter 5).

Isn't it nice to know that, even when you haven't been aware of it, you've been guided by wisdom your whole life? It's good to see wisdom as the ordinary, everyday thing that it is. As you allow yourself to become more and more attuned to wisdom, you may be surprised at just how easily you notice and are guided by it in your life.

Of course, as your understanding of the principles behind clarity deepens, and you're guided more and more by wisdom, it's inevitable that your *experience* of life will get better and better (though you're guaranteed to have ups and downs along the way). And, while people often find themselves getting better results at work and in all areas of their lives, you may also find that some of the things which used to seem important to you, no longer are.

From Coaches to Soapmakers

Two of my clients, Jack and Vivienne, started working with me to help get their coaching business on track alongside their day jobs. As they got a deeper understanding of the principles behind clarity, they experienced an "inner relaxation," and made a startling discovery; they were both passionate about making organic soap! They started researching and experimenting with a sense of joy and ease that was as refreshing as the soap samples they started sharing with their friends. They'd been struggling to make progress on the coaching business, but their passion for the soap business made it easy to do what had to be done. They're now on the verge of moving to the South of France to officially launch their new venture.*

*This mini case study appeared in the first edition of CLARITY. You'll find a ten-year update on Jack and Viv's journey in Chapter 25.

As you allow yourself to be guided by wisdom, you create space for a deeper pattern of life to emerge. As you start living from a deeper understanding of the principles behind clarity, the circumstances of your life move into alignment with your deeper understanding.

So, does that mean that the circumstances of your life are all going to be a bed of roses? Not necessarily. Everyone has hardships to go through and losses to deal with. Furthermore, you don't know if your idea of what a great life looks like today will even *appeal* to you as you live life with a greater clarity of understanding.

So, if we're being guided by wisdom, where does that leave the whole domain of goal setting?

I've got some bad news and some good news for you. . .

keep exploring ✛ connect with others
share your discoveries ✛ deepen your understanding

Thought Experiment: *How good does it feel to realise that you have an incredibly reliable inner guidance system? A means of navigation that's always helping you out with clear, context-sensitive, up-to-the-minute information. . .*

What the Research Says: William Duggan's book, *Strategic Intuition*, looks in depth at the role of insight and intuition in developing strategy (in business, military and other domains). For a taster of his work, you can explore an article he co-wrote with Amy Murphy for *Strategy+Business Magazine*.

As is the case with most of the research referenced in these sections, the article has been written by people who don't have an understanding of the principles behind clarity, so you may need to read between the lines to see our innate capacity for creativity, intuition and insight shining through. You'll find that it's there if you've got eyes for it!

Murphy, A., & Duggan, W. (2020). How to unleash creative thinking. *Strategy+Business* (January 13).

You can access the paper at www.JamieSmart.com/research/Clarity12

Additional Resources

www.JamieSmart.com/Clarity12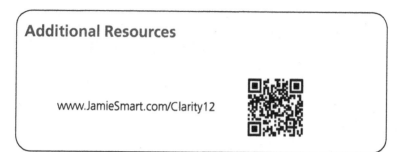

13

Toxic Goals and Authentic Desires

....

"All great things are done for their own sake."

Robert Frost
Poet, playwright

"Escape 9–5, live anywhere, and join the new rich. . ."

I'd been working hard for five years, growing my business, when I read Tim Ferriss' lifestyle-hacking manifesto, *The 4-Hour Work Week*. While I loved the products and services we offered, there was something missing, and I was convinced that Ferriss had put his finger on what it was; I needed to restructure the business so I could spend less time working and more time having adventures!

I met with my team, and we spent months analysing, streamlining and automating. By the next year, I was ready to take my first "mini-retirement"; a three-month holiday to one of the world's premier ski resorts.

"This is it!" I thought as I booked my tickets. "Finally, I'm going to have what I've been looking for. I'm going to be fulfilled, peaceful and exhilarated. I'm going to take my skiing to a new level, feel super-successful and have brilliant bragging rights."

But that's not how it worked out.

After the euphoria of the first week or two on the slopes had passed, I started feeling distracted, uneasy and bored, with a busy mind and sore feet. I was supposed to be on top of the world. Instead, I was in the doldrums! I had the *circumstances* of success, but I wasn't having the *experience* of success.

I flew home six weeks early and went back to the drawing board.

DISTINCTION: Toxic Goals versus Authentic Desires

- **Toxic goals:** Toxic goals diminish a person's quality of life from the moment they set them. They reinforce the outside-in misunderstanding and encourage people to exchange a rich experience of the present moment for contaminated thinking, an idealised future concept.

- **Authentic desires:** Authentic desires are an expression of your innate clarity, wisdom and well-being. They're part of following your curiosity and fascination, things you want for their own sake. As a result, there's no sense of angst or lack with authentic desires, no sense of striving or "I'll be happy when. . . ." When it's an authentic desire, you know you'll be fine whether you achieve it or not.

So am I saying you shouldn't have goals?

No, I'm not. Our neurology uses goal-feedback mechanisms to accomplish even the simplest of tasks, such as scratching an itch, brushing your teeth or making a cup of tea. Goals can be really useful tools for focusing your attention, marshalling your resources, coordinating action and measuring progress. But, just like any other tool, improper use can lead to injury.

Toxic goals often take one of the following forms (you'll recognise some of these as having the "hidden hamster wheel" structure):

- I want [goal] so I can be [happy/peaceful/secure/successful].
- I want [goal] so I can stop feeling [unhappy/insecure/not OK].
- I want [goal] because [I think I should want it/I don't know what I really want/I'm afraid to go for what I really want].
- I want [goal] because I don't want [consequence] to happen.

Goals become toxic when we're believing our experience can come from something *other than* THOUGHT in the moment. People typically respond to toxic goals in one of two ways. They either. . .

- Struggle and strive, failing to achieve the toxic goal (sometimes for years), and finally give up with a sense of frustration and hopelessness, or. . .
- Succeed in achieving the toxic goal, experience an initial rush of euphoria, then feel a sense of emptiness and lack. This is often accompanied by the sentiment *"So that wasn't it either. . .,"* followed by the setting of yet *another* toxic goal (often "bigger and better" than the last one).

The million-pound security blanket

One client I was working with had a goal to raise 2.1 million pounds. He explained that he'd calculated 2.1 million pounds as the amount of money he needed to have in his bank account before he could feel a sense of security. Toxic goal alert! It raises an important question:

How secure can a person ever feel when they're believing their security comes from something "outside", something other than the core of their being?

Many toddlers have a security blanket or teddy bear. Psychologists refer to this as a *transitional object*, something that "gives" the child a sense of comfort and security in times of change or uncertainty (e.g. bedtime). Of course, we know that the blanket or teddy bear can't actually "give" the child a feeling of security or comfort; that can only come from within. It just *seems* to the child as though the feelings come from the transitional object. But it doesn't work that way. It only works one way: inside-out. 100% of the time.

I once worked with a multimillionaire who felt anxious and insecure whenever the stock market dipped. He believed his happiness and security were index-linked! Feelings of security only ever come from THOUGHT, moment to moment, but if a person superstitiously *believes* their security comes from money in the bank, that's the felt experience they'll be living in.

Money is one of the most misunderstood substances on the planet, so many of us have vast amounts of contaminated thinking about it. But money is a tool, a means of storing, exchanging and accounting for value. It can be extremely useful; there are things you can do easily with money that are much more difficult without it. But it's still just a tool, like a hammer or a hairdryer. It has a purpose but, like a hammer or a hairdryer, money can't deliver something beyond the scope of its functions. Specifically, it can't give you a feeling of security; that can only ever come from within.

Reality Check

When I first alert people to the issue of toxic goals, they sometimes object, saying something like *"But if I'm happy and get my sense of security from within, how am I ever going to be motivated to do anything? If I didn't think my goals would bring me the feelings I want, I won't have any drive."*

One of the great myths of our culture is that if people don't have a sense of *lack*, they won't be motivated to do anything. But it's not true. In Daniel Pink's book *Drive* (a study of motivation) he points out that money (for instance) *isn't* a motivator – that while "not enough" money can demotivate people, big cash incentives actually *decrease* performance on cognitive and creative tasks. He suggests that in the workplace (for instance), sustaining high levels of motivation is a function of autonomy, mastery and a sense of purpose.

Every adult knows that the child's security blanket involves a trick of the mind, but how often do we look to adult "teddy bears" (e.g. jobs, possessions, money, relationships) as though they're somehow different? There's nothing wrong with material success. But you're much more likely to enjoy it when you build it on your sense of *inner* security and *true* peace of mind.

Remember: Toxic goals are just contaminated thoughts. You weren't born thinking them, and you were motivated to learn to walk and to talk. You were motivated to use your hands, to play and to explore. You were motivated to make and create, to love and connect with other people. And you still are, whether you're already aware of it or not.

A Tale of Two Automobiles

One of my clients, Carl Harvey, was thrilled the day he bought his new car. The Mazda MX5 convertible with leather seats and all the trimmings had been a dream of his for ages. But when we met for lunch a couple of weeks later, he was downhearted. He explained that, while he'd been over the moon for the first few days after he bought the car, the initial euphoria had been replaced by a strange emptiness, and a craving for something bigger and better. He told me that he'd believed this car was going to make him happy, but it turned out that he probably needed a Ferrari. As I spoke to Carl about the *"I'll be happy when. . ."* trap, and explained how THOUGHT creates our experience of reality, something shifted for him. He had an insight, and his experience of the car was transformed. The craving disappeared, and was replaced with a lasting appreciation and enjoyment. A few months later, Carl got offered an opportunity in Australia, and he delighted in giving the car to his younger brother as a gift. Carl moved to Sydney, where he splits his workdays between consulting in the city and running an online business from his apartment overlooking Bondi Beach.*

Allan, a successful business consultant, attended one of my events. During a follow-up conversation, I asked what differences he'd noticed since the workshop. He said "It's been weird." When I asked for details, Allan explained that, throughout his career, he'd used various material goals to motivate himself. Even as we spoke, above his desk was a picture of the luxury automobile he'd been planning to treat himself to when he hit his next financial target. *"The strange thing is,"* he said, *"since your workshop, I don't really care about that car anymore. In fact, I think I'd rather get a bicycle and ride to work."* He'd started to see through a misunderstanding, and something shifted for him. Allan was still just as inspired to reach his business goals, but no longer needed the car to motivate him.

* This mini case study appeared in the first edition of *CLARITY*. You'll find a ten-year update on Carl's journey in Chapter 25.

Authentic desires

So, if the outside-in misunderstanding sponsors toxic goals, what kind of goals are sponsored by an inside-out understanding of life? How can we relate to goals in a way that is fulfilling, productive and healthy?

Case Study: Authentic Desire, Vision and Direction

Joe Stumpf had spent 20 years building an incredibly successful business, *"By Referral only,"* providing support to real estate agents and mortgage brokers in the US. Every month, for the previous two decades, he'd flown to a different town or city to run a bootcamp to help agents and brokers start getting their businesses on track. Not only were these events the first step in Joe's sales and marketing funnel; Joe also saw himself as a torch bearer, bringing knowledge and hope to people who, when they first met him, were often struggling to make a living. His business specialised in helping them move out of struggle and into stability and success (many of Joe's formerly struggling clients go on to serve as de facto mentors to others). Joe asked me to coach him because he was at a point of transition and was feeling stuck. He was proud of the business he'd created, but he no longer wished to fly from city to city each month. He knew that phase of his business was finished, but didn't know what the next phase was. He wanted a new vision for his business and himself, so I worked with Joe to help him find clarity. He emerged with an inspiring vision for his business and for his role in it. Joe says *"The insights I gleaned from our session resulted in one of the most important directional shifts of my life."* Joe's business has shifted to being not just a training company, but to also being an information publisher and service provider. It's continued to go from strength to strength. And, just as important, Joe's following his heart and living life on his own terms. He took on the challenge of being the oldest man ever to survive the civilian version of the navy seal "Hell Week," and he's written a book called *Willing Warrior*.

One of the great things about authentic desires is that they don't need to be realistic; you want what you want, whether you believe it's possible for you or not. When you discover an authentic desire, you may have no idea how you're going to achieve it. That's OK. The Pulitzer prize–winning author, E. L. Doctorow once said:

> *Writing is like driving at night in the fog. You can only see as far as your headlights, but you can make the whole trip that way.*

We can extend the fog metaphor by thinking of authentic desire as a beacon in the distance. When you step into the fog of the unknown, and keep moving forward, wisdom will guide you in discovering the path (the "how"). To put it simply, *Clarity plus Action equals Results*.

CLARITY plus **ACTION** equals **RESULTS**

Figure 13.1 The Clarity Results Model

Reality Check

What about targets, goals and objectives set by other people – my boss, for instance? He sets me toxic goals all the time, but I don't have the luxury of replacing them with authentic desires.

Another person can set you a goal that you don't *like*, but the only thing that can make it toxic is contaminated thinking: the idea that *your* happiness, security or peace of mind is in some way bound up in it. You may say, *"But I have to do it or I'll lose my job – it's like having a gun to my head."*

The idea that your happiness, security or well-being are dependent on you keeping your job is a great example of the outside-in misunderstanding. Looking to a job for security is like looking to a toaster for peace of mind. It's not that jobs and toasters aren't useful; they just can't give you what you can only find within. One of the things you'll begin to notice as you continue deepening your understanding of the principles behind clarity is that tasks that used to bother you become less and less of an issue. If you're willing to make space for your authentic desires, and take action, you'll be amazed at where they will lead you.

Once you realise your clarity, security and well-being aren't dependent on setting or achieving goals, you can relax, and allow wisdom to guide you. As you begin to see you don't need *anything* to be OK, you also realise there's no urgent need to uncover your authentic desires; they'll emerge in their own time.

In the meantime, stay in the game. Eighty percent of success is showing up, and authentic desires often find you where and when you least expect it.

So, with that in mind, I'd like to take you somewhere very special, to a place that holds the answers to all your questions, and the solutions to all your problems. . .

keep exploring ❖ connect with others
share your discoveries ❖ deepen your understanding

Thought Experiment: *As you're reading this now, are there any toxic goals that still look like a reality to you? By contrast, what are some of the authentic desires that you're already starting to become aware of?*

What the Research Says: In Chapter 7 of my book *RESULTS*, I talk about the famous Yale University study of 1953. A generation of motivational speakers used the study as an endorsement of goal setting, claiming that the 3% of the class who had clear written goals and a plan for achieving them were more successful 20 years later than the other 97% of the class combined. *Fast Company* magazine conducted an investigation of the claims and the Yale University archives were searched thoroughly but no trace of the 1953 study could be found. Yale University has since stated categorically that no such study of the class of 1953 ever occurred.

Fast Company. (2012). Why setting goals could wreck your life. (Nov. 9).

You can read the article at www.JamieSmart.com/research/Clarity13

Additional Resources

www.JamieSmart.com/Clarity13

14

The Power of Presence

....

"We convince by our presence."

Walt Whitman
Poet and journalist

"It's. . . Uhh. . . Ahh. . . Umm. . ."

The location was St Lucia, and it was the third day of one of my Life Transformation Retreats. One of the participants had just had a profound insight (signalled with a loud "OH!" and a look of sudden realisation). Everyone in the group turned to him, eager to hear about the pearl of wisdom that had just been revealed to him. He opened his mouth to speak and said *"It's. . . uhh. . . ahh. . . umm. . ."* He stopped, furrowed his brow, then tried again. This time, no sounds came out; his mouth just opened and closed as the expression on his face cycled through a variety of emotions: surprise, confusion, puzzlement, amusement, peace. . .

His contaminated thinking had been massively interrupted; he'd woken up to the present moment.

Being present

Being present is often described as having your attention on what's happening in the present moment. But there's more to it (and less to it) than that. . .

"Present" is whatever is happening moment to moment, prior to your habitual thinking.

Our experience of life is inherently clear, fulfilling and involving when there's nothing else in the way. What gets in the way is our habitual patterns of contaminated thinking. For example. . .

A. A person can be in a situation they might normally describe as "wonderful," but be having an experience that is stressed, anxious or miserable because they've got something on their mind. An all-too-common example of this is when people go on holiday. They can be in the most beautiful environment, with the people they most want to be with, but they find their work has come on holiday with them, thanks to their habitual patterns of thinking.

B. By the same token, a person can be in a situation they might normally describe as "boring" or "miserable," but be having an experience that is rich, fulfilling and profound because they've got nothing on their mind. I sometimes enjoy sitting by the ocean, looking out at the waves for 20 or 30 minutes at a time. Twenty years ago, I would have had enough of it after two minutes and felt bored and distracted if I had to stay there. But because I have less on my mind these days, the experience of the waves is rich, absorbing and engaging (except when it's not).

What's the difference between the two situations? In situation A the person is caught up in contaminated thinking, while in situation B the person has greater clarity; the principle of THOUGHT is creating a rich experience of the moment, relatively unperturbed by contaminated thinking.

So, how does our habitual thinking take us out of the present moment? By creating THOUGHT-generated "objects" that transport us into the future or the past. These THOUGHT-generated objects can take a variety of forms, for example:

- Toxic goals
- Worrying
- Anxiety
- Daydreaming
- Resentments

- Remembering
- Ruminating
- Judgements
- Imagining
- Planning

- Fear of loss
- Comparing
- Validation-seeking
- Attention-seeking
- And so on

But here's the thing:

There is only ever this moment. The present is all there is. . .
The future and the past are THOUGHT-generated illusions. . .
Illusions that you only ever experience in the here
and now. . .

Thought Experiment

Try this out: Remember an enjoyable experience from the past. One hundred percent of your experience of that memory is taking place in the present moment; none of it is happening in the past. Now imagine something you're going to do in the future. One hundred percent of your experience of that imagined event is taking place in the present moment; none of it is happening in the future. When you find yourself in the "now," it's an indication that you're not caught up in habitual thinking; you've "fallen awake" to the present moment.

Case Study: Grace under Pressure

Tim is an entrepreneur with several successful businesses and was used to experiencing all the stress and pressure that can bring. Then he started exploring the principles behind clarity, and he found himself becoming increasingly present, patient and resourceful. As he started having insights into where the stress and pressure were actually coming from, they began to reduce. He now stays calm in situations that used to aggravate him, and it's paying off; Tim's work involves a lot of high-value negotiations, and his calm new demeanour has been worth many tens of thousands of pounds in deals done and contracts won. And it's equally valuable in situations of growth and crisis. When one of Tim's businesses lost a contract worth 50% of its annual sales, the more traditional reactions of panic and stress were nowhere to be seen. Instead, his calm assessment allowed a rapid and positive response to the challenges posed. Tim was able to reduce the scale of the loss and quickly find replacement orders. Tim said, *"Feeling calm and being able to handle pressure is priceless, but bills don't pay themselves. What's really great is the fact that I can put a financial value on this understanding."*

DISTINCTION: Meditating versus Meditation

The act of **meditating** is a practice that has one goal: entering a state of **meditation**. Meditation is a reflective state that's often accompanied by a sense of clarity and peace of mind, free from contaminated thinking, and resting in the present moment. ("A state of meditation" is another way of describing the reflective states that give rise to the flashes of strategic brilliance mentioned in Chapter 12.)

Contrary to popular opinion, you don't need to be meditating in order to enter a state of meditation. People find themselves in a state of meditation in a variety of situations: going for a walk, listening to classical music, fishing, running, taking a shower, driving, listening to another person, sitting in quiet reflection, reading a book and so on.

As you continue exploring these principles, you'll start finding your way into a state of meditation, free from contaminated thinking, more and more frequently. So does this mean you'll find yourself cross-legged, chanting "Ommm" in the middle of business meetings? Fortunately not.

Just as realisations are context-sensitive, so is clarity. The meditative states you find yourself enjoying will be fit for purpose, bringing you what you need, when you need it.

The athlete's clarity (aka "the zone") when they're performing at their best has a different flavour to the computer programmer's clarity (aka "flow"). While they're both expressions of clarity, they're configured to meet different requirements. They're different again from the tranquil, meditative state that arises when you're getting away from it all, looking at the sunset, the ocean or little fluffy clouds. But all have three things in common: clarity of thought, access to the resources you need and being present to the moment.

Your deepening understanding of the principles behind clarity will bring you more and more fully into the present, with everything you need to respond effectively in the moment.

In Chapter 13, I suggested that the present holds the answers to all your questions and the solutions to all your problems, and you may be wondering if this bold claim is justified. How is finding your way back to the present going to make a difference to the things that matter in life? Here's how. . . Do you remember the Bateson quote?

The major problems in the world are the result of the difference between how nature works and the way people think.

When you fall awake from contaminated thinking, you're more closely aligned with reality. When you're in the present, you're responsive to what's happening, with the clarity that comes from being aware of your deeper connection with life.

A person's thinking is what's behind their ability to perceive something as a problem in the *first* place. When you step into the present, you step out of your habitual ways of seeing a situation. This liberates you to tune in to wisdom and see reality more clearly.

Clear mind, more time

One of the things I often hear from my clients when they start exploring the principles behind clarity is how much more time they have. Whenever a client says this, I make a point of asking what they attribute this extra time to. Their answer usually includes one or more of the following points:

- The amount of time they're no longer wasting in insecure, outside-in thinking.
- They have realisations that lead to more effective use of their time.
- They experience more intuitive decision-making, with less time wasted stressing about choices.
- They find more elegant, leveraged ways of getting things done and achieving results.
- They come up with better ideas and creative solutions to problems.
- They eliminate tasks that no longer seem important.
- They find less time is lost to worry and anxiety and more time is spent in a flow state.
- They get more from the time they spend and are more productive.
- They perform better, resulting in greater impact, fewer errors and less rework.
- They think less about what they're going to do, procrastinate less and act more.
- They have a richer experience of the present moment, getting more "juice" from their day.

> *The outside-in misunderstanding is the biggest time thief there is. If it wasn't for contaminated thinking, we'd discover that every day brings a 1:1 match of time and enterprise. When we're present, with a clear mind, we have what we need for the task at hand. We intuitively know when to pause and when to press on, when to rest and when to proceed. . .*

This doesn't necessarily mean that on a daily basis you're going to work out at the gym, respond to all your messages and clear your to-do list. Your judgements about what you *should* be doing are not necessarily part of this 1:1 match of time and enterprise. But as you continue to explore the principles behind clarity, you'll discover the implicit connection between presence, performance and perfect timing.

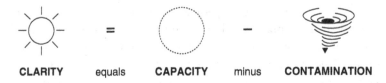

| CLARITY | equals | CAPACITY | minus | CONTAMINATION |

When you fall out of habitual thinking and into the present, you slip out of the outside-in misunderstanding about how life works. The idea that your well-being is being held hostage by a given problem or issue often drops away, and clarity emerges. Strange as it may seem, you discover that all is well in this moment.

Reality Check

You may be saying *"What about problems that need solving urgently? If I lose my job, clarity isn't going to help me pay the bills!"* Life has its ups and downs. While some hardships are inevitable for each of us, there are two things that enable us to deal with any situation we encounter:

1. We each have within us a source of security, resilience and well-being.
2. We each have within us a source of clarity, wisdom and guidance.

In fact, these things aren't just *within* you; they *are* you. Clarity, wisdom and resilience are expressions of your *true nature*. The knowledge that clarity comes from within, combined with your innate guidance system gives you everything you need to deal with the ups and downs of life.

All over the world, on a daily basis, people lose jobs, get divorced, lose loved ones and get injured. We all get dealt our share of hurts, hardships and disappointments. People's responses to these misfortunes range from denial, trauma and shutdown to reflection, acceptance and bounce back. As Sydney Banks put it. . .

> *Life is like any other contact sport; you're going to*
> *get your knocks. But it's not the knocks that count;*
> *it's how you handle them.*

When you have clarity, you realise you have what you need to respond appropriately and deal with what comes your way.

A lot of the things that people experience as "problems" are grounded in contaminated thinking, an outside-in *misunderstanding* of reality. The stress and anxiety inherent in this misunderstanding has people creating problems where there are none and responding unresourcefully to the things that *do* need dealing with.

Fortunately, there's something utterly reliable that everyone's got, but that very few people *realise* they have. Something that means you don't need to worry, that you've got what it takes to handle what comes your way. . .

---

keep exploring ❖ connect with others
share your discoveries ❖ deepen your understanding

Thought Experiment: *"If it wasn't for contaminated thinking, we'd discover that every day brings a 1:1 match of time and enterprise."* Consider this curious statement. Then reflect on the assertion that, if it weren't for contaminated thinking, you'd find every activity you undertake to be engaging, absorbing and fulfilling.

What the Research Says: In a widely cited paper, "The Power of Presence," researchers conducted a study into the effect of the state of mindfulness at work. They describe mindfulness as "a positive psychological state" and "a state of consciousness in which individuals pay attention to the present moment with an accepting and nonjudgmental attitude."

Note that the researchers were attending to the *state* of mindfulness rather than the practice of any mindfulness techniques or approaches. They used a measure that has been "explicitly designed to assess mindfulness in the general population in samples with no explicit experience with mindfulness training or meditation." Their conclusion was as follows:

Our research revealed that mindfulness facilitates the recovery process in two ways. At the day level, mindfulness experienced during work positively relates to psychological detachment after work and sleep quality in the following night. At the week level, our findings revealed that employees high on mindfulness are less susceptible to effects of entrainment and display constant high levels of psychological detachment over the work week.

Hülsheger, U. R., Lang, J.W.B., Depenbrock, F., Fehrmann, C., Zijlstra, F.R.H., & Alberts, H.J.E. M. (2014). The power of presence: The role of mindfulness at work for daily levels and change trajectories of psychological detachment and sleep quality. *Journal of Applied Psychology, 99*(6), 1113–1128.

You can access the paper at www.JamieSmart.com/research/Clarity14

Additional Resources

www.JamieSmart.com/Clarity14

15

Resilience

....

*"Our greatest glory is not in never falling,
but in rising every time we fall."*

Confucius
Philosopher

"There's no place like home . . . there's no place like home. . ."

In the film *The Wizard of Oz*, the heroine (Dorothy, played
by Judy Garland) gets caught in a tornado and wakes up in the
strange land of Oz. She's desperate to find her way home to Kansas
and goes on a quest to meet the wizard whom she believes holds
the key to her return.

At the end of the story, Dorothy discovers she has the power
she needs *within* her. She taps her ruby slippers together, repeats
the phrase, *"There's no place like home"* and wakes up in her bed,
surrounded by her family. Dorothy doesn't believe them when they
first tell her the adventure in Oz was a nightmare. She protests that
it was a real place, but they reassure her that she never left her
home; that it was just a dream. . .

We've all had the experience of waking up from a dream so realistic we thought it had actually happened, felt the sense of gratitude and relief as the racing pulse of nightmare gives way to the reality of the here and now. The dream reality seems so real that we *mistake* it for a material reality. But all along, the dreamer is tucked up in bed, sleeping soundly, perfectly safe.

Touching the Void

The nerve-shredding documentary, *Touching the Void*, tells the story of Joe Simpson and Simon Yates, two climbers who made the first ever ascent of the west face of Siula Grande in the Peruvian Andes. On their way back down, Simpson fell and broke his leg. It was a death sentence. Simpson told Yates to go on without him, but Yates refused, instead choosing to lower him down the steep, snow-covered slope at the end of a long rope. After hours of painstaking descent, Yates suddenly felt the rope go taught; Simpson had fallen and was hanging off the edge of a cliff!

Yates was stuck in a nightmarish dilemma. Simpson's weight was slowly pulling Yates free from his belay point in the snow. If Yates kept holding on, they'd both be pulled off the mountain, but the only alternative was to cut the rope.

Finally Yates made a decision; he cut the rope and Simpson plummeted into a crevasse where he lay shivering and alone, without food and seriously injured.

When Yates climbed down and saw the crevasse, he assumed his friend was dead and continued down the mountain. But Simpson was alive. Over the next three days, in a feat of resilience that can only be described as heroic, Simpson hopped, crawled and dragged himself over treacherous terrain, arriving at the base camp only hours before Yates was due to leave.

In Simpson's description of the incident, he explained that it wasn't "him" that brought him down the mountain; it was as if *someone else* was doing it. That "someone else" was innate resilience, a power we all have.

Sleepwalking

A huge number of people today "sleepwalk" through life, inno-cently hypnotised by the outside-in misunderstanding. Occasion-ally they wake up to a deeper, more profound experience in the moment, but they usually attribute it to some aspect of their cir-cumstances before going back to business as usual. In fact, we all sleepwalk some of the time, no matter how "awake" we may be. We all fall into the outside-in trance on a regular basis – that's part of what it is to be human.

We walk around with our heads in fog, lost in a world of con-taminated thinking. But, all the time, the ground we are walking on is a world of clarity and depth of experience, a more profound sense of peace and understanding. No matter how real and compelling our perceptual realities sometimes seem, a world of deeper experi-ence is just below the surface, in every moment.

Sometimes, the outside-in hypnosis is so powerful, it seems un-believable that clarity and peace of mind could be so nearby. We mistakenly believe that our ability to reconnect with them can be in-fluenced by material-world factors; factors such as the length of time we've been thinking and feeling in a certain way, the intensity of our feelings or the difficulty we've had solving a problem until now.

We assume our thought forms have the same qualities as the material world, but they don't. They're made of THOUGHT, the real-ity principle, fleeting and ephemeral, literally the stuff that *dreams* are made of. Clarity and well-being are always there, always within reach, no matter how distant they may have seemed until now.

A Tale of Two Burglaries

Years ago, I caught a young man trying to rob my offices. He managed to slip out the fire escape and I gave chase, but he outran me. Despite the fact that he hadn't managed to steal anything, I was upset and, as the day went on, I felt more and more angry. Finally, I called one of my mentors, Terry, and asked for his help. I said I couldn't understand why I was getting so angry, but I wanted it to stop. What he said will stay with me forever.

You've got a business model, and that young man has a business model.
Your business model has certain advantages and disadvantages, and so
does his. For a start, his model probably involves him running away from
angry people more often than yours does.

In the blink of an eye, I saw the whole situation differently. My spirits rose and I started feeling peaceful. I was no longer angry at the young man.

Clarity and peace of mind have a natural buoyancy. Like a football being held underwater (as mentioned in Chapter 9), as soon as you let go, it rises to the surface. It doesn't matter how long you've been holding it there, or how much effort you've put into it; the moment you let go, its natural buoyancy begins to lift it. And, just as a football's natural buoyancy is an implication of the principle of gravity, clarity and resilience are implications of the principles of MIND, THOUGHT and CONSCIOUSNESS.

One night, two years later, I arrived at my home to find the front door hanging open; my house had been broken into and my laptop and mobile phone stolen. To my amazement, I was calm, philosophical and practical. I did what I needed to do, without fear, anger or agitation. The realisation I'd had two years previously was still serving me.

When we're lost in contaminated thinking, we sometimes experience feelings of worry, agitation, urgency and so on. Due to a trick of the mind, we tend to "blame" those low feelings on something *other than* the principle of THOUGHT in the moment. As soon as we do that, we give our power away and feel we urgently need to solve our problems, achieve our goals and make changes in our lives.

The worse we feel, the more urgent and compelling those external changes can seem.

But, as clarity emerges, we wake up to a deeper, more connected experience of life. Suddenly the things we'd been perceiving as problems look different; they disappear, we see obvious solutions or just feel confident that we'll find a way forward. Creativity comes to the surface, and our natural resourcefulness and resilience come into play. We intuitively know that we'll be OK no matter what and that we can trust wisdom to guide us.

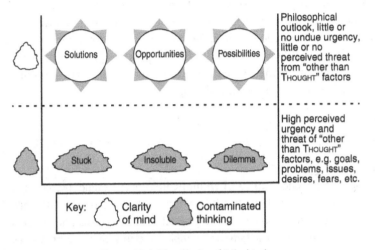

Figure 15.1 The Clarity of Mind Index

Reality Check

Am I suggesting that you stick your head in the sand and ignore your problems? No! But I *am* suggesting that your ability to perceive something as a problem in the *first place* is an expression of habitual thinking and your level of understanding. As you see the situation more clearly, everything looks different, including what you'd been perceiving as a problem.

We've all experienced this. We struggle with an issue for hours, days or even longer, then one morning we wake up and either (1) we no longer experience it as a problem, or (2) we see a solution that seems *so* obvious, we can't believe we didn't think of it sooner. You are innately resilient; clarity, perspective and peace of mind are always there, just one realisation away.

And what may seem counterintuitive in our modern world of multitasking, instant messaging and 24-hour opening is this: You can live with and from clarity, insight and a more profound felt experience of life. Everyone gets hoodwinked by contaminated thinking from time to time, and no one gets to avoid its lows completely. The outside-in misunderstanding is compelling, and our moods inevitably go up and down. But greater clarity and a richer experience of life are our natural state, so we can start to gravitate towards that as our default setting.

DISTINCTION: Clarity of Thought versus Clarity of Understanding

We all experience **clarity of thought** from time to time, present and in the moment, with our heads free from contaminated thinking. While the flow states regularly enjoyed by athletes, musicians and dancers (among others) are a familiar example of clarity of thought, we all experience this in different ways and at various times in our own lives. Clarity of thought, by its nature, is somewhat fleeting; no one has it all the time.

Clarity of understanding is the degree to which you *insightfully* understand the inside-out nature of reality, your embodied understanding of the principles behind clarity. The fact that you're reading this book means that you're in the process of becoming one of those exceptional people who is developing clarity of understanding about the inside-out nature of life. An increase in your clarity of understanding is developed one realisation at a time and is permanent. Once you experience an increase in your level of embodied understanding, you never lose it. You'll lose sight of it from time to time (if you're anything like me, it'll be on a daily basis), but your insights into the inside-out nature of life are still there within you; it's only a matter of time before wisdom guides you back to clarity.

Of course, we all have an innate understanding of the inside-out nature of life at the core of our being; these principles are what we're made of at the most essential level. So, as you keep looking in this direction, and allowing realisations to dissolve the outside-in misunderstanding, it's inevitable that your clarity of understanding will continue rising. And the higher it rises, the more clarity of thought you'll find yourself experiencing.

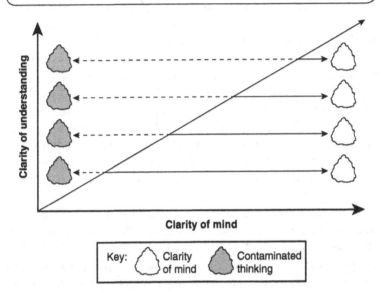

Figure 15.2 Clarity of Mind versus Clarity of Understanding

Life is not a problem to be solved

The philosopher Kierkegaard wisely remarked that life is not a problem to be solved; it's a mystery to be experienced. When we lose our clarity of thought, we innocently look at life as a series of problems to be solved and goals to be achieved. But the agitation and urgency are actually wisdom signals. . .

- Reminding us that we're living in the experience of the principle of THOUGHT taking form in this very moment. . .
- Pointing us in the direction of clarity, possibility and peace of mind. . .

- Guiding us to look away from the *content* of our experience and towards that which is *creating* our moment to moment experience, the formless principles of MIND, THOUGHT and CONSCIOUSNESS. . .

As you start to see how these principles are playing out in your life (and always have been), you can start living more and more in clarity, insight and a deeper felt experience of life. You'll still have your ups and downs, but behind them is the knowledge of resilience and the default setting of innate clarity and well-being.

Near the end of *The Wizard of Oz*, Glinda the good witch reveals that Dorothy has *always* had the power to get home but that she wouldn't have believed it if she'd been told at the beginning; she had to discover it for herself. When asked what she's learned, Dorothy says *"If I ever go looking for my heart's desire again, I won't look any further than my own backyard. Because if it isn't there, I never really lost it to begin with!"*

You'll find that contaminated thinking tends to be about "me and my circumstances" (How am I doing? What do I need? How do I look to others? What if I lose this? How can I get that? I'll be happy when. . ./I can't be happy because. . . and so on). It looks real, so you get fooled into searching and seeking outside yourself for something that's already there within. When we get caught up in contaminated thinking, we innocently mistake it for a material reality. But it's not a reality – it's just a dream.

The dream reality seems so real that we mistake it for a material reality. But, all along, the dreamer is tucked up in bed, sleeping soundly, perfectly safe. Everyone has dreams of isolation and insecurity from time to time but, in any moment, you can wake up to the reality of who you really are. . .

- You are the dreamer. . .
- You are the thinker. . .
- You are not the dream; you are what's *dreaming* the dream. . .
- You are not your thoughts; you are what's *creating* the thoughts. . .

You are not your experience;
you are what's creating your experience;
MIND, the power principle,
the intelligent energy behind life. . .

In any moment, you can wake up to the truth of who you really are and live life more fully from clarity, realisation and peace of mind. . .

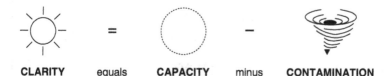

CLARITY equals **CAPACITY** minus **CONTAMINATION**

So, if the dream of isolation is an illusion, what's the deeper reality behind life? If you are the dreamer, perfectly safe, what's the truth of the domain you're resting in? And what awaits you as you continue waking up?

Keep exploring ⁂ connect with others
share your discoveries ⁂ deepen your understanding

Thought Experiment: *Isn't it a relief to realise that clarity, security and peace of mind are always on hand? Ready to rise to the surface, no matter what, as soon as you insightfully realise that you're living in the experience of the principle of THOUGHT taking form in this very moment?*

What the Research Says: The phenomenon of post-traumatic stress disorder (PTSD) is commonplace, but a less well-known area of study is that of post-traumatic growth. Nietzsche's aphorism – "What doesn't kill me, makes me stronger" – resonates because it points to a truth that people have been aware of since ancient times: People often grow and transform in incredibly positive ways in the aftermath of distressing events.

In the *Handbook of Posttraumatic Growth: Research and Practice*, researchers Calhoun and Tedeschi feature a variety of papers looking at posttraumatic growth in a variety of contexts, including children, holocaust survivors, disaster and emergency workers, cancer survivors and more.

Calhoun, L. G., & Tedeschi, R. G. (2014). *Handbook of Posttraumatic Growth: Research and Practice*. Psychology Press.

You can access the handbook at
www.JamieSmart.com/research/Clarity15

Additional Resources

www.JamieSmart.com/Clarity15

16

Connection and Relationships

....

"Despite our habit of seeing ourselves as separate, solid 'things,' our minds, our beings are not fixed. We exist in a web of relationships."

Joseph Jaworski
Author and founder of
The American Leadership Forum

"Make me one with everything. . ."

The punchline to the old joke about the Buddhist and the hotdog vendor casts a light on one of life's most persistent illusions. It certainly can seem like we're separate from each other and from the natural world. But, strange as it may seem, there's a way in which the *experience* of separation is an illusion. In reality, the fact that everything is made of energy means, in a very empirical sense, we are all connected: with one another and with the rest of the universe.

We don't need anyone or anything to "make us" one with everything. We already *are* one with everything; we always have been and we always will be. However. . .

Contaminated thinking creates the experience of separation.

As we get caught up in contaminated thinking, we experience the *illusion* of separation from other people, and from life. The more contaminated thinking we're in, the more separate we feel.

And what does this have to do with connection and relationships?

The true source of loneliness, isolation and most conflict is the mistaken belief that we're feeling something other than THOUGHT *taking form in the moment, that we're at the mercy of a world "out there" with power over how we feel.*

The *experience* of connection is incredibly valuable. In addition to the fact that it's natural and feels good, connection opens up a conduit for effective communication. When another person feels connected to you, they're much more likely to see where you're coming from, hear what you have to say, feel well understood and be impacted by what you're sharing with them.

Connection, intimacy and love are what's already there for us when there's nothing else in the way. . .

So what gets in the way? Habitual patterns of contaminated thinking.

CLARITY equals **CAPACITY** minus **CONTAMINATION**

Listening to be impacted

A few years ago, I was at a meeting where one of the participants asked for help with an issue he'd been struggling with. He gave a brief outline of the problem (he'd been having trouble finding the right direction for his business), then the other participants started jumping in with solutions. I just listened. When the first round of solution giving was over, I asked if it would be OK to do some exploring. He and the other participants agreed, so I asked him questions, then listened as deeply as I could to his answers. A feeling of connection started to develop, and he became reflective. All of a sudden, his face lit up. *"I need to have more passion and adventure in what I'm doing,"* he said. Over the weeks and months that followed, he started making the necessary changes to move in a new direction.

When you listen deeply, and allow a connection to emerge, the resulting conversations can be profound, creative and extremely useful.

The London Olympics

During the London Olympics, a curious phenomenon took place; all over the country, people's moods lifted. I was interviewed by *Sky News* to give my perspective. At one point, the interviewer asked why communities were coming together around the Olympics and why people felt more connected to one another. I said that feelings of connection and belonging are natural for people when they're not lost in isolated, stressful thinking; that when people feel more connected, they have a greater sense of well-being. I explained that there's nothing inherent in events such as the Olympics that has us feeling connected or disconnected; it's always down to the power of THOUGHT.

It looked like the Olympics was making people feel more optimistic and connected, but the optimism and connection they were feeling came from *within*; the experience of connection is *natural* for people when they're less caught up in contaminated thinking.

As your understanding of these principles continues increasing, contaminated thinking falls away and you start experiencing greater connection in all your relationships. . .

 = −

CLARITY   equals   **CAPACITY**   minus   **CONTAMINATION**

Case Study: Rapid Development

Ian works as a programme manager for a disruptive online business. The company employs 400 people and has an aggressive development schedule, releasing new versions of its online services several times per month. Ian runs two teams of extremely bright, talented individuals (many of them honours graduates from Oxford and Cambridge), and he's responsible for new software releases. It's a fast-moving enterprise, using agile, "just in time" development processes.

Before Ian started learning about the principles behind clarity, the high-pressure, high-speed environment was stressful and hyper-busy, making life difficult for him and his team members. There were entrenched viewpoints and antagonistic differences of opinion. Communications broke down easily; project timescales were affected and the results were less than ideal. Ian tried to use various techniques to get people aligned, but nothing seemed to be working.

Then Ian joined one of my programmes and started learning these principles. Over the course of 12 months, a trust developed between the individual team members and with the business stakeholders. He reported that there was more engagement, honesty and open communications. Ian went on to explain that, while his team still apply analytical thinking and solid business experience, the principles behind clarity provide a stable foundation for those efforts. Ian says, "It's still hard work, and issues come up, but they get sorted out quickly now."

In the past, a dispute between a team member and a business stakeholder raged on for a year and was only resolved when the team member was physically moved out of the team. By contrast, a recent dispute that had the potential to go the same way was solved by Ian over a few conversations in less than 48 hours; now the two people work well together. Ian explains, "There's a better feeling in the team, with more learning during our weekly review sessions. People really listen to each other these days." The team members are more playful, yet both teams have hit all their deadlines with high-quality results. Ian conservatively estimates the bottom-line impact of what he's been learning at over £300,000 in improved delivery times alone.

* This mini case study appeared in the first edition of CLARITY. You'll find a ten-year update on Ian's journey in Chapter 25.

Two worlds in one

Imagine you're watching a film at the cinema. As you look at the characters on the screen, you experience them as separate people – figures moving against a background. Our ability to experience them as distinct from each other (and from the background) is what allows us to transform the patterns of light on the screen into individual characters. This in turn allows us to experience the drama of the film as it unfolds.

But the seemingly separate figures on the screen are actually part of an unbroken continuum of light and shadow. The distinctions between the characters, and between figure and ground, are mind-made illusions, generated from within us. The same goes for all the feelings we experience as we watch the movie.

*The film is neutral; 100% of our experience of
(and response to) the film arises from within.*

Now, let's go one step further. The flow of images on the screen is only there because light is shining from a projector at the back of the cinema. The patterns of light on the screen have no existence independent of the projector and the reel of film it's playing. Form and formless are one, a unified whole. Switch off the light and the movie disappears from the screen.

*The tangible illusion of the film on the screen has no
existence separate from the (relatively intangible) reality
of the light shining from the projector.*

It's the same with us. Our experience of the world of form (including each other) is a tangible illusion: tangible, but not real. The principles behind clarity represent a deeper reality: intangible, but utterly real, giving rise to the tangible illusion of the material world. And get this: The images on the screen have no existence independent of the light from the projector. . .

Just as a wave has no existence separate from the ocean. . .
The material world of form in all its glory has no existence
separate from the formless energy behind life. . .
Form and formless are one, a unified whole. . .

Leading physicists such as David Bohm (one of the pioneers of quantum mechanics) acknowledge that an understanding of the oneness of life is essential for science and humanity to continue evolving.

In a dream, your mind creates and perceives a world. . .

When you're asleep and dreaming, all the characters, environments and situations are created from *within*. It's the same when you're awake. Remember: 100% of your experience of the world "outside" of you is actually taking place on the *inside*, generated from deep within your consciousness (albeit with a live data stream via your senses). The principles behind clarity give rise to our experience of reality.

As our clarity of understanding increases, something amazing begins to happen. Life starts looking less complex, and we begin to see a simplicity behind many of the challenges people face. In fact, in a world that appears beset by a dizzying array of complex issues and seemingly impossible problems, there's a realisation that can offer genuine hope and practical solutions. . .

---

keep exploring ⁖ connect with others
share your discoveries ⁖ deepen your understanding

Thought Experiment: *"Connection, intimacy and love are what's already there for us when there's nothing else in the way." What would it mean for you and your various relationships if this were true?*

What the Research Says: In his extraordinary book *Wholeness and the Implicate Order*, quantum physicist David Bohm offers a model describing the nature of reality. He explains that the truth of reality

---

is wholeness, that the world of form we experience – which he calls the *explicate order* – emerges from (and is contained within) a deeper, formless reality: the implicate order.

Bohm uses the metaphor of the vortices (whirlpools and eddies) in a flowing river. While the vortices may appear to be relatively stable, "existing" over an extended period of time at a specific location, they have no existence separate to that of the flowing river.

Just as a wave has no existence separate from the ocean, the material world of form (the explicate order) in all its glory has no existence separate from the formless (the implicate order).

Our personal thoughts, perceptions and self-images are like Bohm's vortices; we can notice them, obsess about them, even take ownership of them. But they have no existence separate from the whole. They don't "belong" to us any more than a droplet of water "belongs" to a given whirlpool or wave.

A fascinating recording was made of David Bohm discussing this with the scientist David Suzuki in 1979.

Bohm, D. (1980). *Wholeness and the implicate order*. Routledge Classics.

You can find the interview here:
www.JamieSmart.com/research/Clarity16

Additional Resources

www.JamieSmart.com/Clarity16

PART THREE

The Way Forward

17

There's Only One Problem

....

"When I am working on a problem, I never think about beauty but when I have finished, if the solution is not beautiful, I know it is wrong."

R. Buckminster Fuller
Designer and inventor

"Behind the London riots a multitude of causes. . ."

The *Euronews* headline from August 9, 2011, attempted to make sense of the riots that had started that week in London (sparked by the tragic shooting of Mark Duggan by police marksmen), then spread to other cities in the UK. The "causes" identified in the days that followed ranged from poor parenting and gang culture to budget cuts, social media and consumerism.

In response to the litany of causes came a variety of proposed solutions. Then British Prime Minister, David Cameron, promised an "all-out war on gangs and gang culture." Police responded by arresting 200 gang leaders; but the strategy backfired, creating a dangerous power vacuum. Younger, more volatile gang members stepped in to fill their shoes, leading to an increase in violence, mayhem and chaos.

But what if this dizzying array of societal, family and individual "causes" were actually not causes, but effects: *the emergent properties of a single, underlying cause?*

The Lime Solution

During the early 1800s, countless women were dying of puerperal fever, a bacterial infection contracted during childbirth. At the time, the illness was attributed to a mind-boggling variety of causes (ranging from bad smells, "atmospheres" and inclement weather to posture during labour, psychological factors and even *constipation*).

In the 1840s, a Hungarian doctor, Ignaz Semmelweis, noticed that women who gave birth at home, in the midwives' ward or even in the street had a much *lower* incidence of puerperal fever than those who gave birth in the doctors' ward of his hospital. He had a sudden realisation: the illness was being spread by something invisible on the hands and instruments of the doctors.

In May 1847, Semmelweis ordered that all staff in his hospital wash their hands in a chlorinated lime solution before contact with the patients. The rate of puerperal fever fell from 18% to less than 3%.

The theories of the day had identified dozens of "causes," but there was in fact just one cause: bacteria on the doctors' unwashed hands and instruments.

Today, every doctor knows the importance of scrubbing up, wearing correct surgical attire and sterilising their instruments. One of the legacies of Semmelweis's discovery is that most people today survive routine surgery, most of the time.

Semmelweis was less fortunate; despite the massive success of the procedures he instituted, his discoveries disagreed with the theories of the day. The medical orthodoxy thought Semmelweis's discovery was too simplistic, lacked credibility and offended their sensibilities (the doctors didn't like the implication that their hands were dirty). He was at first ridiculed, then violently opposed, losing his job and being committed to a mental asylum where he died in 1865 of septicaemia. Semmelweis's practice of handwashing didn't become widespread until many decades after his death.

Is it credible that a single cause is responsible for the London riots, just as a single cause was responsible for puerperal fever? If so, what could possibly explain such a diverse and complex array of effects?

A misunderstanding: the innocent belief that we're feeling something *other than* the principle of THOUGHT in the moment. This misunderstanding leads to contaminated thinking just as surely as a misunderstanding about germs leads to contaminated surgical instruments. For example:

- If a person believes their feelings of security come from money, then neediness, greediness or both are understandable responses.
- If a person believes their agitated feelings are caused by other people, then they're likely to experience resentment, hostility and other relationship problems.
- If a person's habitual thinking is standing between them and their deeper feelings of peace and well-being, then they're likely to feel unhappy or unfulfilled.
- If a person doesn't understand that 100% of their felt experience is coming from THOUGHT in the moment, then stress is a strong possibility.
- If a person doesn't realise they have a source of wisdom within, and they make important decisions when they're clouded with contaminated thinking, they're going to make some bad decisions.
- If a person doesn't realise that they are profoundly resilient, and they see trouble on the horizon, then they're likely to worry.

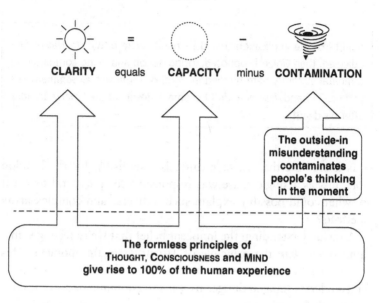

Figure 17.1 Contamination: The Outside-in Misunderstanding

It doesn't take a huge leap of creativity to trace most of the day's news topics to a small number of culprits: neediness, greed, anxiety, stress, anger, resentment and lack of wisdom. And all these culprits are symptoms of a single problem: contaminated thinking resulting from the outside-in misunderstanding.

The theories of the day had identified dozens of "causes," but there was in fact just one cause. . .

Everyone wants to have a more connected, vibrant and fulfilling experience of life, whether they realise it or not. When we believe our *felt experience* is threatened by something other than THOUGHT, we'll do almost anything to avoid those perceived causes (e.g. the number of people who would *literally* rather die than stand up in front of a group and speak in public). When we believe our *felt experience* is provided by something other than THOUGHT, we'll do almost anything to bring those circumstances into being (e.g. the family man who torpedoes his career, wrecks his marriage and drains his bank account to run off with his secretary, because he believes she's the source of his happiness and well-being).

As people begin waking up to the inside-out nature of life, they naturally start living from a more alive, more profound felt experience. It becomes your home base. When contaminated thinking pulls your attention away from that deeper experience of life, it's rarely long before wisdom wakes you up to the fact that you're living in a THOUGHT-generated perceptual reality, and the system continues self-correcting.

When clarity of thought is grounded in clarity of understanding, it's the natural source of the behaviours traditionally associated with "high character." As you have realisations into the inside-out nature of reality, and reconnect with that more profound experience of aliveness, you naturally start responding to situations with clarity, wisdom and integrity.

Reality Check

You may be saying "What about things like natural disasters, unavoidable accidents, diseases and dementia? There are lots of problems that *aren't* down to contaminated thinking!"

True. Life has its ups and downs, and no one gets through it without their share of challenges. Seeing the inside-out nature of reality and living from a clearer, more profound experience of life won't stop that. But it gives us (1) the resilience to know we can deal with whatever comes our way, and (2) the wisdom, clarity and creativity to make a difference in our own lives and in the lives of others going forward.

It turns out that life is less about what happens to you, and more about how you relate to it. . .

In the past 100 years alone, realisations have resulted in innovations that have made a massive difference in the lives of millions. Alexander Fleming's discovery of penicillin in 1928 has resulted in countless people being saved from killer infections.

But what if there was a kind of "penicillin for the mind" that could have as dramatic an effect on your clarity, your character and your behaviour as antibiotics have had on bacterial infection?

---

keep exploring ⁂ connect with others
share your discoveries ⁂ deepen your understanding

Thought Experiment: *What happens when you consider the possibility that the vast majority of the problems faced by society, businesses and individuals are the result of a single cause? A misunderstanding of the nature of THOUGHT?*

What the Research Says: *The New England Journal of Medicine (NEJM) is one of the most prestigious medical journals in the world (in the same league as The Lancet, The Journal of the American Medical Association and the British Medical Journal). It is also one of the oldest medical journals, having published consistently since the early 1800s. As such, it gives us a unique perspective on how our world has changed over the past two centuries.*

In my book RESULTS, I reference an article published in the April 1817 issue of the NEJM, as follows:

An 1817 issue of the highly esteemed New England Journal of Medicine included an article called "Practical Remarks on Some of the Predisposing Causes, and Prevention, of Puerperal Fever, with Cases." Puerperal fever (aka "childbed fever") was a hideous infection afflicting one in four women who gave birth in hospitals during the eighteenth and nineteenth centuries, often resulting in the death of mother and infant. The race was on to identify the causes, and the article listed a wide variety, ranging from constipation and vigorous exercise to long journeys and the weather.

The list of spurious causes was accompanied by a list of spurious preventative measures, including avoiding exercise, avoiding bodily motion, reducing food intake, hastening delivery, inducing vomiting and bloodletting. The one true cause (bacteria) and the appropriate preventative measures (antiseptic procedures) were missing. Why? Because the role of germs in causing illness was not understood. Doctors of the day routinely carried out autopsies then conducted internal examinations on pregnant women without first washing their hands.

Channing, W. (1817). Practical remarks on some of the predisposing causes, and prevention, of puerperal fever, with cases. *New England Journal of Medicine, 6,* 157–169.

You can find the article at www.JamieSmart.com/research/Clarity17

Additional Resources

www.JamieSmart.com/Clarity17

18

Penicillin for the Mind

....

"No problem can be solved from the same level of consciousness that created it."

Albert Einstein
Physicist, winner of the Nobel Prize in Physics, 1921

"There's nothing in this world that you can't turn into heroin. . ."

During an unexpectedly moving scene in the comedy *Get Him to the Greek*, drug-addicted rock star Aldous Snow (played by Russell Brand) tries to convince his ex-girlfriend Jackie Q (played by Rose Byrne) to get back together with him. She explains that she's drug-free and that the past few months have been the happiest of her life. He protests that he was clean for seven years when they were together. She replies *"And you did yoga for five hours a day. That's mental! There's nothing in this world that you can't turn into heroin."*

"Symptom substitution" is widely accepted in the world of traditional addiction treatment. The smoker gives up cigarettes but starts eating chocolate. The reformed cocaine addict becomes a workaholic. The alcoholic stops drinking and starts compulsively attending meetings. The surface behaviour has changed, often to something less damaging, but the habitual thought patterns (and the level of understanding underpinning them) remain the same. By the same token, we can all think of examples of people who have had a sudden realisation: a change of heart that dramatically and positively affects their life. . .

- The alcoholic who experiences a "moment of clarity," stops drinking for good and becomes a valuable member of their community
- The smoker who suddenly decides that "enough is enough" and easily gives up a habit they were previously enslaved by
- The workaholic businessman who has a heart attack, massively re-evaluates his priorities, downsizes and starts working a four-hour day so he can spend more time with his family

These changes of heart are often regarded as psychological anomalies, sometimes labelled as "spontaneous remission" and given no further attention. Yet they are examples of a natural quality that we all have:

The capacity for realisations that lead to an increase in our clarity of understanding, a rise in our level of consciousness.

The infinite elevator

Imagine a sturdy, see-through elevator running up the side of an infinitely tall skyscraper at the centre of a crowded metropolis. When you first step into the elevator, all you can see is the cars at street level and the buildings that surround you.

As the elevator begins to move, you start rising above the smaller buildings, and your sight line becomes less cluttered. The cars appear to grow smaller and smaller, and you can see the rooftops of the neighbouring office blocks. Soon, all but the tallest buildings are disappearing beneath you, and you can see far into the distance.

You admire the gentle transition as the population becomes less dense: from high rises, to low rises, to suburbs, to countryside. As you continue your upward journey, the details of the city streets shrink into invisibility, and your eye is drawn to the sweep of the horizon. Eventually you start to become aware of the curvature of the Earth.

Your consciousness is like this infinite elevator. A rise in consciousness means an increase in clarity of understanding that brings you peace, perspective and greater clarity of mind.

The principle of CONSCIOUSNESS brings your THOUGHT-generated perceptual reality to life. When you experience a rise in your level of consciousness, the habits of thinking you previously experienced as a reality suddenly start losing their power. As your consciousness continues rising, you become more and more able to see your THOUGHT-generated perceptual realities for the illusions that they are.

> *A rise in consciousness is a* permanent *increase*
> *in your clarity of understanding. . .*

Penicillin for the mind

A rise in consciousness is like a kind of penicillin for the mind. Penicillin can help our bodies to heal infection by inhibiting the growth and spread of illness-causing bacteria. Similarly, a rise in consciousness can transform how we relate to (and can even eliminate) huge amounts of contaminated thinking. A person whose consciousness rises often experiences an across the board increase in well-being, with issues they'd been perceiving as problems suddenly reducing in intensity, or even disappearing. . .

Case Study: Fear of Conflict and Public Speaking

Tiffany was afraid to express her point of view during meetings at work, particularly if there was negativity or if she disagreed with the points others were making. She joined one of my programmes, and we chatted about the principles behind clarity. The following week she found herself able to speak freely during her team meeting, even though she knew other people disagreed with her. She even gave a presentation to the group (something she'd been avoiding doing for months due to a fear of public speaking). Tiffany told me afterwards that she found the presentation so straightforward that she couldn't understand why she'd ever thought it was a problem. She had an insight – a rise in her level of understanding – and her innate clarity, resilience and well-being took care of the rest. It acted where it was needed.

DISTINCTION: Achievement Obsession versus Understanding Orientation

- **Achievement obsession:** If a person believes we live in an outside-in world, it's logical for them to be achievement obsessed: to focus tirelessly on achieving goals and eliminating problems.
- **Understanding orientation:** Once a person has even an *inkling* that we live in an inside-out world, it makes sense to adopt an understanding orientation; you recognise that your embodied understanding of how life works is your biggest leverage point in whatever you want to accomplish.

Here's a way of thinking about it. Imagine two doctors living in London in the 1850s. Doctor A believes that illness and disease are caused by bad smells. He spends every available hour on a scheme to supply highly scented flowers to every hospital ward in the city. He's totally focused on this *achievement*, because he wants the best for his patients. Doctor B is looking in a different direction. He's heard suggestions that illness and disease aren't caused by bad smells, but rather by tiny invisible creatures called germs and bacteria. He spends his time exploring this new *understanding*, because he wants the best for his patients.

Paradoxically, when you start to shift to an understanding orientation, it often raises the bar on what you're able to achieve. I've seen this in my own life and in the lives of my clients: many of your biggest achievements come after you let go of an achievement obsession, and start increasing your clarity of understanding.

People are often surprised as the things they have been perceiving as "problems" diminish in intensity or disappear. Mountains get turned back into molehills, and people find they have the resources to tackle the things that do need dealing with, guided by innate wisdom.

With subtractive psychology, a person or organisation will still have goals they want to achieve and problems they want to solve, but their attention is oriented towards a more leveraged understanding of life. All too often, the things people perceive as problems and issues, wants and needs, are merely a reflection of their contaminated thinking in the first place. An increase in your clarity of understanding can radically transform the way you relate to what you had been perceiving as important. You may start to notice yourself becoming more accepting of your weaknesses and imperfections, while finding healthy ways to mitigate them.

Case Study: Taking the Pressure Off

Kevin came from a high-pressure corporate background, where he felt he had to strive for the same things his colleagues wanted (flash cars, expensive suits, champagne, luxury watches, etc.). When he started exploring the principles behind clarity, Kevin had some powerful increases in understanding, and his whole landscape changed. He discovered that it's OK for him to be himself. Previously he'd been uncomfortable with the thought of living abroad, but he decided to experiment with moving to Central Europe. He's not wasting his energy; instead, he's taking the time to live life in a way that feels authentic and true to him. He says that he's experiencing a real sense of purpose, but without any sense of pressure. Kevin now gets huge enjoyment from the simpler things in life; his work as an internet marketer leaves him plenty of time to explore his new surroundings and meet new people. Kevin's clarity of understanding isn't just giving him more happiness and well-being in his life; it's also helping him to follow his wisdom and do things in ways that work for him.

The achievement obsession is about optimising results and solving problems at your existing level of consciousness. The understanding orientation is about experiencing a rise in your level of consciousness. While the rise often results in significant achievements and other benefits, they are side effects: positive by-products of the deeper understanding.

Case Study: Looking for the Formula

Bec was brought to one of my events by a friend. She told me later that, during the event, she had a nice feeling and thought the subject matter was interesting, but she wasn't aware of any huge insights. In the weeks that followed, however, it was a different story. Up until then, Bec had been approaching her business in a formulaic way, but that no longer felt right for her. She stopped looking outside herself for "the right way" to do things and got more connected with innate wisdom. She told me that it was like being introduced to a "her" that had been hidden away for a long time, a Bec that knows she's going to be OK no matter what.

She says *"My life has moved from being rigid and conventional to a place where I'm willing to play with the unknown and allow for some amazing new possibilities."* While she still gets hoodwinked by contaminated thinking from time to time, she's realising more and more quickly that it's just that: thinking. Bec explains, *"When this happens, I sit down, slow down, and wait for clarity. And it comes; it always comes."* And the difference isn't just showing up in her own life; it's having an impact on the way she relates to other people: her children, her clients, her partner. Her formulaic "problem" wasn't something that she'd been looking to solve, but it was causing her unnecessary stress and pressure, so wisdom gave her what she needed.

Once again: One of the dangers of the achievement obsession is that the process of achieving from that mindset can actually *reinforce* the outside-in misunderstanding, the mistaken belief that our THOUGHT-generated *perceptual* reality is in fact a *material* reality, and that our clarity, security and well-being is in some way dependent on it.

Reality Check

Am I saying there's anything wrong with wanting to achieve things? No, I'm not! But there's a huge difference between achievement that's driven by the sense of need and lack (the *"I'll be happy when"* of contaminated thinking) and the achievement that comes as a natural expression of following the inner guidance of wisdom and inspiration, secure in the knowledge that you are *already* enough.

The Morphine of Self-improvement

Outside my window stands a strong, healthy tree, about 40 feet tall. Many years ago, a seed was planted in the ground, and it started growing. The roots reach down into the nourishing soil, creating a strong foundation; the leaves absorb sunlight and carbon dioxide, transforming them into life-giving nutrients; the branches and leaves drink in the falling rain. The tree continues growing.

The tree doesn't "work on" growing. It just grows. Growing is its nature.

There's a way in which our attempts to "take control" of our personal evolution can actually interfere with our natural propensity to grow. The seeker's habitual searching is the very thing that stands in the way of them finding what they yearn for. Like an opiate, the intoxicating patterns of struggle and striving numb their emotional pain, while blinding them to the natural joy of living.

There's nothing in this world that you can't turn into heroin. . .

But, like the tree in my garden, growing is your nature. Clarity of understanding releases the self-love, gratitude and acceptance that are the sunlight, rainwater and nutrients of your personal evolution. While you don't get to decide the timescale, increases in consciousness and clarity of understanding are *inevitable* for you when you get out of your own way, let wisdom guide you and start enjoying your life as it is today.

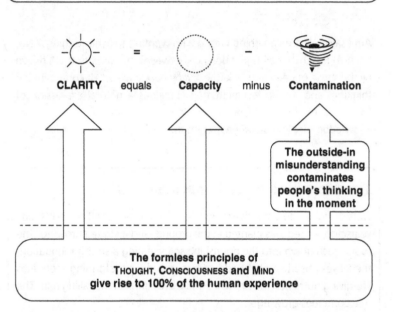

I realise that an understanding orientation might seem like a counterintuitive choice for someone living in the "real world" of work, families, goals, businesses, mortgages, health and relationships. But as you pay attention to that inner wisdom and keep increasing your understanding of the inside-out nature of life, you're going to be guided in living a life you love, no matter what.

So what do you need to do in order for that to happen?

keep exploring ⟡ *connect with others*
share your discoveries ⟡ *deepen your understanding*

Thought Experiment: *What would happen if you decided not to treat yourself as a "thing" to be improved and instead open to the possibility that it's your nature to continue learning, growing and evolving?*

What the Research Says: "All for One and One for All: Mental Disorders in One Dimension" (534 citations) is the title of a research paper published in the *American Journal of Psychiatry* (April 2018). In it, authors Caspi and Moffat suggest that "empirical evidence has now accrued to suggest that a single dimension is able to measure a person's liability to mental disorder, comorbidity among disorders, persistence of disorders over time, and severity of symptoms." They term this single dimension p and draw conceptual parallels with the g factor of general intelligence (i.e. p is to psychopathology severity as g is to mental ability).

"A New 'Inside-Out' Perspective on General Factor p" is an article written as a comment on Caspi and Moffat's paper and published in *European Psychiatry* (the official journal of the European Psychiatric Association). It was written by my colleagues Thomas Kelley, Dr William F Pettit Jr, Jack Pransky and Judith Sedgeman, who make the following claim:

Just as there is an innate health-producing design behind every human system (i.e., gastro-intestinal, cardio-vascular, excretory) we posit there is also an innate health-generating design behind the agency of thought; that virtually everyone is born thinking in an effortless, free-flowing way and experiencing mental health.

In a 2018 conversation I had with Dr Pettit, he suggested a single dimension u representing a person's level of understanding, effectively expressing a complementary position to dimension p that Caspi and Moffat posit.

Caspi, A., & Moffitt, T. E. (2018). All for one and one for all: Mental disorders in one dimension. The American Journal of Psychiatry, 175(9), 831–844. https://doi.org/10.1176/appi.ajp.2018.17121383

Kelley, T., Pettit, W., Pransky, J., & Sedgeman, J. (2019). A new "inside-out" perspective on general factor *p*. *European Psychiatry, 61*, 85–87. doi:10.1016/j.eurpsy.2019.06.009

You can access the Caspi & Moffitt article here:
www.JamieSmart.com/research/Clarity18

Additional Resources

www.JamieSmart.com/Clarity18

19

Do Nothing

....

"The Master doesn't try to be powerful; thus he is truly powerful. The ordinary man keeps reaching for power; thus he never has enough. The Master does nothing, yet he leaves nothing undone. The ordinary man is always doing things, yet many more are left to be done."

Lao Tze
Philosopher

"Point yourself in the right direction and do nothing. . ."

Sydney Banks' provocative statement seemed to fly in the face of everything I "knew" about how to live an inspiring, successful life. It raised questions. . .

- What's the "right" direction, and how do you know when you're pointed in that direction?
- If you're "doing nothing," how does anything ever get done?
- How is this even helpful?

Yet, while it was easy for the thrash metal band of my habitual thinking to raise objections to the statement, I could also feel a truth in it. After all, I was a master of "doing"; I'd accomplished a lot in my life by taking action, but a lot of my "doing" had me running on the hamster wheel of *"I'll be happy when. . ."* thinking.

My explorations had introduced me to the curious notion of "not doing." The idea of a more effortless approach to life was certainly appealing to me, but the idea of pointing myself in the right direction and "doing nothing" still sounded like a recipe for inertia, passivity and, ultimately, disaster, particularly in today's fast-moving, fast-changing business environment.

But it turns out that just because you're "doing nothing" doesn't mean that nothing gets done. . .

DISTINCTION: Misguided Action versus Inspired Action

- **Misguided action** is action sponsored by the mistaken belief that it will lead to results that either give a person the *felt experience* they desire or stop them from experiencing the feelings which they want to avoid. The contaminated thinking behind misguided action is often tinged with striving, urgency and desperation.

- **Inspired action** is action taken from the clarity of the inside-out understanding: the knowledge (at least intuitively) that your felt experience can't be threatened or delivered by anything other than THOUGHT; that you are psychologically safe. Acting from this clarity is the essence of high performance, what athletes, dancers and musicians sometimes refer to as being in flow. When people say things like *"I felt a sense of calm, and suddenly I just knew exactly what to do,"* what often follows inspired action.

When a person is acting from clarity, they'll still have powerful intuitions about the importance of timing, but there's rarely a feeling of stressful urgency. That's one of the reasons inspired action can be so effective and impactful.

Point yourself in the right direction and do nothing. . .

So what are the answers to the questions raised by this curious statement?

What's the "right" direction, and how do you know when you're pointed in that direction?

Pointing yourself in the right direction means looking towards what's *creating* your experience of life, looking to the *source* rather than the *contents* of your experience.

And what's creating your experience of life? The principles behind clarity.

When we're caught up in contaminated thinking, we're fixated on the *form* of life. Our THOUGHT-generated perceptual reality always *seems* real, so it can feel as though we really should be obsessing about whatever it is we're thinking about. When we're seeing how life *really* works (inside-out), we move back towards clarity and are in a better position to be guided by wisdom.

In any moment, we can turn our gaze from the *content* of our experience (what we're thinking about) to what's *creating* our experience (the principles of THOUGHT, MIND and CONSCIOUSNESS).

If you're "doing nothing," how does anything ever get done?

"Doing nothing" isn't about the actions you *take* so much as it is about the mindset that gives *rise* to your actions.

Most people spend much of their lives taking misguided action: "doing" from contaminated thinking and the feelings of stress and urgency that often come with it. When you're "doing nothing," your actions are sponsored by clarity and understanding.

So does that mean you should only take action when you're seeing clearly? Definitely not.

Stay in the Game

Woody Allen famously said that 80% of success is showing up. While it's great to feel intrinsically motivated, take inspired action and get into the zone, it's surprising how often the inspiration waits until you're already in the game before it shows up.

My dear friend and colleague, *Stillpower* author Garret Kramer, works with senior executives and professional athletes to help them improve performance and get the results they desire. Neither group has the luxury of sitting around waiting for inspiration to strike – they need to show up, ready to work when their team needs them. Whether they're seeing things clearly or lost in contaminated thinking, Garret's advice is the same: Stay in the game!

And why stay in the game? Because, as I said in Chapter 4, the mind is context-sensitive. Subtractive psychology points to an extraordinary "intelligence" capable of giving you what you need when you need it. When you stay in the game, and allow your mind to self-correct, your head will clear, and you'll be given what you need to deliver the goods. This is in stark contrast to the person who sits on the sidelines (literally or metaphorically), trying to "get their head right," waiting until they "feel ready." I know people who have been waiting for so long to "feel ready" that they've become experts at waiting (not a promising field of expertise).

When I first got the invitation to appear live on national TV, my contaminated thinking had me squirming and looking for a way out of it. Fortunately, I understood what was happening, so I stayed in the game and showed up. It's the same in everyone's life. When we follow the dubious advice of our insecure, outside-in thinking, we're stuck in "Groundhog Day," repeating the habits of the past and re-creating what we no longer want.

When we're willing to show up, despite our insecurities,
we create new possibilities.

While inspired action feels great, sometimes you just need to "do the right thing," in spite of your contaminated thinking. As you continue allowing yourself to become more responsive to wisdom, you'll often find that the answers you need come at the exact moment you need them.

Sometimes the "right thing to do" is to take a specific action.

Sometimes the "right thing to do" is to stop and take a rest.

Sometimes the "right thing to do" is to wait for further guidance. In the meantime, stay in the game!

People love closure, the feeling of "knowing" and being right. But, if we're willing to spend some time "not knowing" and looking to the unknown, the results are often remarkable. If you're willing to wait, wisdom will often provide an answer very quickly. At other times it may take longer, but the more you're willing to "not know," the more you'll realise how many things aren't actually as urgent as we sometimes pretend.

But what about those times when you need to make a decision immediately, and you're not getting a clear steer from wisdom one way or another? In those situations, you make the best decision you can based on the information available. These are exactly the moments when the best thing you've got going for you is clarity. When all other factors are equal, the person with the clearest head is holding the strongest hand.

How is this helpful?

In Chapter 9, I explained that our understanding of how life works has more influence than any other factor over our experience of life, and the results we get. This is particularly important when it comes to the actions we take, because. . .

People always do what makes sense to them based on their embodied understanding of reality (aka their level of consciousness). Every action a person takes is consistent with their understanding of how life works (even if they can't explain why that's so):

- The CEO works an 80-hour week because it makes sense to them.
- The athlete trains hard because it makes sense to them.
- The alcoholic drinks because it makes sense to them.
- The manager checks their email every ten minutes because it makes sense to them.

- The devout worshipper attends church because it makes sense to them.
- The surgeon masters their craft because it makes sense to them.
- The criminal robs a bank because it makes sense to them.
- The student stays up late studying for their exam because it makes sense to them.
- The OCD sufferer washes their hands for the 50th time that day because it makes sense to them.
- And so on. . .

The actions we take are informed by our understanding of how life works and serve to reinforce that understanding. When we act from the outside-in misunderstanding, the actions we take reinforce that (mis)understanding. When we act from an inside-out understanding of life, the actions we take endorse that understanding. Even if it's the same action!

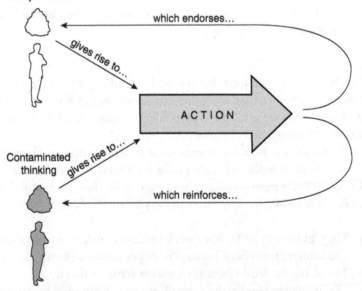

Figure 19.1 Actions Endorse/Reinforce Understanding

Of course, the goggles we're looking through colour how we perceive our lives. . .

- People who worry a lot find no shortage of things to worry about.
- People who are easily satisfied tend to be contented and enjoy what they have.
- People who think there's somewhere to get to and that "there" is better than "here" don't tend to spend much time enjoying the present moment.
- People without much on their mind tend to have a rich experience of life.
- A person who consistently acts from contaminated thinking will tend to have an experience of life that reflects their lack of understanding.
- A person who consistently acts from clarity, guided by wisdom and an inside-out understanding, will tend to have an experience of life that reflects their clarity of understanding.

Reality Check

But if the actions a person takes reinforce their understanding of how life works, doesn't that mean that people will "be happy when" they get the things they think will make them happy? Sadly not. The actions reinforce their understanding, but life only works one way: inside-out. What typically happens to people on the hidden hamster wheel is that they either

- Prevent themselves from getting what they want, or
- Get what they want, experience a temporary high, then feel deflated, going "I guess that wasn't it after all – now I need to figure out what I *really* want."

In both these cases, the "I'll be happy when. . ." superstition stays intact.

So, when you're staying in the game, leaving your thinking to self-correct and increasing your clarity of understanding, a world of new possibilities starts opening up for you. Your increasing enjoyment in leading your own life may even inspire you to start guiding others in this direction. Either way, it's worth getting the inside track on. . .

---

keep exploring ❖ connect with others
share your discoveries ❖ deepen your understanding

Thought Experiment: *How would your life be different moving forward if you were willing to show up and stay in the game, regardless of any contaminated thinking you may have?*

What the Research Says: In Chapter 11 of my book *RESULTS*, I wrote about the record-breaking sprinter Usain Bolt and how he avoids the visualisations and pre-race routines favoured by his competitors. Instead, Bolt has fun connecting with the crowd before the race, explaining, "I try to make people laugh and enjoy everything I do." When asked why he favours this approach he said, 'I've learned over the years that if you think too much about a race you just make yourself more nervous."

> Lawton, M. (2015). Usain Bolt reveals his desire to be the greatest athlete of all time. . . ahead of his sporting heroes Muhammad Ali, Michael Jordan and Michael Johnson. *Daily Mail.* (13 February).

You can read the interview at
www.JamieSmart.com/research/Clarity19

Additional Resources

www.JamieSmart.com/Clarity19

20

The Leadership Delusion

....

"Leaders don't create followers,
they create more leaders."

Ralph Nader
Attorney consumer advocate and political activist

"Here's the problem: Our business is growing steadily at 25%.
We're taking on new staff every year, but we haven't found a
way to develop new leaders at anything *like* the same rate. . ."

I was speaking with the practice manager for a consulting group
that works with Global 1000 companies. His comments echo
a sentiment I've heard repeatedly from company directors over
the years, "We need more leaders; they're hard to find and even
harder to make!"

A recent search for the term *leadership* on Amazon returned
93,606 books. All over the world, people attend programmes,
read books and listen to audios, trying to master the skills and
qualities of leadership.

But if the 93,606 books were looking in the right direction, don't you think we would have found the solution to "the leadership problem" by now?

A group I was working with were exploring the subject of leadership. I invited them to make a list of what they considered the causes of leadership to be. The list they came up with included these qualities:

- Vision
- Passion
- Goals
- Contribution
- Flexibility
- Listening
- Being decisive
- Stillness
- Action
- Teambuilding

While the items they'd identified are certainly valuable, they're actually symptoms or "effects" of the leadership bug, rather than the causes.

DISTINCTION: Symptoms versus Causes

- **Symptoms:** Most leadership books and programmes make a valiant effort to help people master the "symptoms" of leadership – behaviours, skills and attitudes – modelled from successful leaders. Unfortunately, acting like you have the symptoms of leadership is similar to acting like you have a cold: difficult and unconvincing.
- **Causes:** The source of leadership is the cause that gives rise to the symptoms. As you start to catch the "leadership bug," you'll find the symptoms of authentic leadership start emerging effortlessly and authentically.

So what causes leadership? What's the bug that gives rise to these symptoms? And how does a person catch it? I've got some good news, some bad news and some great news:

- **Good news:** You've already got it; everyone has the "cause" of leadership within them.
- **Bad news:** For most people it's covered over, shrouded in layers of contaminated thinking.
- **Great news:** As you increase your clarity of understanding, you awaken your innate capacity for leadership.

Highway Mirage

Sometimes, when you're driving on a hot day, you see a mirage on the road ahead, an optical illusion that looks like a pool of water.

The first time you see one, it's a little strange, but you quickly learn that there's no pool of water in the road. It's just a mirage – an illusion – so you don't need to take any evasive action.

Like the flat earth, the geocentric universe, and the miasma theory of disease, contaminated thinking has no grounding in reality. Instead, it's grounded in the mistaken belief that we can feel something other than THOUGHT in the moment. But that belief is 100% false; it doesn't work that way.

And, like a mirage, contaminated thinking is just an illusion, so you don't need to take any evasive action when you notice it. Understanding its nature is enough.

The "deep drivers" described in Chapter 4 are the expressions of your innate capacity for leadership. As you begin to see past your contaminated thinking, the deep drivers shine through, and the "symptoms" of leadership start showing up. This is what's going on when people say that an individual has "character."

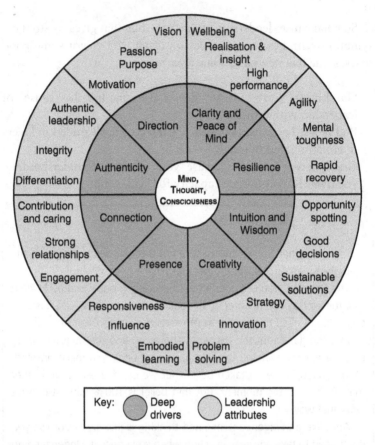

Figure 20.1 The Principles Drive Leadership Attributes

Take a moment to contrast some of the attributes of clarity with those of contaminated thinking:

Attributes of contaminated thinking	Attributes of clarity
Clouded, repetitive, clogged	Clear, fresh, free-flowing
Unresponsive, stuck in the past	Responsive, present, in the moment
Change-averse, inflexible, rigid	Agile, flexible, open to change

Attributes of contaminated thinking	Attributes of clarity
Serious, insecure, boring	Playful, confident, fun
Tense, preoccupied, struggling to learn	Relaxed, alert, learns quickly and easily
Traumatised, weak, helpless	Resilient, tough, persistent
False, fake, defended, closed	Authentic, real, transparent, open, unique
Flat, dull, repetitive, unmotiv-ated, passive	Passionate, inspired, purposeful, motivated, proactive
Fearful, anxious, worried	Fearless, curious, experimental
Isolated, separate, lonely, shut down	Connected, warm, listening, loving
Self-centred, harsh, cruel	Understanding, kind, compassionate
Stressed, taking things personally	Peace of mind, philosophical, reflective
Dissatisfied, sense of lack, needy, greedy	Appreciative, grateful, contented, giving
Reactive, habitual, indecisive	Intuitive, guided by wisdom, decisive
Stale, habitual, closed	Creative, innovative, open to new ideas

Feel free to add your own distinctions to this list. The fact is, when we're lost in contaminated thinking, we can't help but show up on the left side of the list. But the moment we realise that it's just a mirage, we're on our way back to the right side.

If only I knew how. . .

One of the most common laments I hear from people is this:

I'd follow my dreams and do what I want to do, but I don't know how.

This is contaminated thinking. Despite the sale of millions of copies of "How to. . ." books and programmes, very few people take action and put what they learn into practice. The "How to. . ." book has usually been written by someone who accomplished something of value, then shared the symptoms of their accomplishment (but not the causes). If the symptoms are like apples, the causes are the tree that grew them. When people buy "How to" books and programmes, they're usually trying to glue someone else's apples onto their tree, without realising it doesn't work that way! Think about it: To accomplish something of value and write a "How to. . ." book, you likely have to do the following:

- Take responsibility for yourself and your results.
- Clarify your sense of direction, and find your authentic voice.
- Step into the spotlight, and risk criticism and/or failure.
- Look within yourself for security, resilience and persistence.
- Hone your intuition and strengthen your decision-making muscles.
- Develop your creative process and discover the how-tos that fit for you.

These are some of the key elements of leadership. But the "How to" book can't give you these; you have to grow your own. When you look to someone else to tell you how to do what's right for you, you're accidentally giving your power away, implying that they know and you don't. Programmes that teach the how-tos of leadership without an understanding of the underlying causes are subtly reinforcing the "follower" mindset.

Why is it like this?

A Compliant Workforce

The Industrial Revolution created a huge need for a compliant workforce to operate the factories, but there was a problem. Most of the workers were accustomed to seasonal work relating to farming and crop cycles. The regimented timetable of factory life was foreign to them, and when they had amassed enough money to pay for a few days' worth of food and drink, many of them would stop coming to work.

This caused a huge problem for the factory owners, who needed consistency of production. So they exerted pressure for the introduction of mandatory schooling and gave generous donations to the clergy, whose sermons started including messages about the nobility of labour, the importance of obedience and "an honest day's work for an honest day's pay." The school system was designed along factory lines to create good workers: consistent, obedient, conditioned.

It didn't have much effect on the first generation of factory workers. It was only when their *children* arrived for work that the strategy started playing out. For over 200 years, the majority of people have internalised huge amounts of contaminated thinking telling them there's a right way of doing things, that they don't know what it is and that someone in authority needs to tell them the answer. As a result, many (most?) people have become dependent on others to tell them what to do in at least some important aspects of their lives.

Arguably, this kind of conditioning was necessary for our stage of development in the 1800s, but it's way past its sell-by date today. The challenges being faced by modern businesses require all the clarity, creativity, and agility we can muster. We need leaders who are willing to take responsibility, decisions, risks and action.

Thought Experiment

Stop for a moment and have a guess at how much of your working life has been spent lost in contaminated thinking. Now have a guess at how much of your colleagues' working lives have been spent lost in it. Now have a guess at the number of unnecessary conflicts, missed deadlines and botched jobs have come from all that contaminated thinking. Now have a guess at all the sick days and stress-induced illnesses that have resulted from it. Now multiply it by all the businesses in the country, in the world.

To an individual, to a business, to the entire economy, the cost of contaminated thinking is *astronomical*, not just in terms of lost productivity and unnecessary problems, but in terms of squandered energy, unused creativity and missed opportunities.

Fortunately, as you continue increasing your understanding of the principles behind clarity, you'll find your innate leadership capacities emerging and developing. This creates a strong platform for you to lead from, to create from and to learn from. You see, as you develop your leadership capacities, you can learn from any person, book or programme. You intuitively know what's right for you, taking what fits and leaving what doesn't. And this doesn't just apply to leadership. . .

Beating the bell curve

Here are some of the more popular soft skills courses that companies and individuals invest in:

Leadership skills	Personal development	HR management
Management skills	Sales and marketing	Change management
Coaching skills	Conflict resolution	Time management
Negotiation skills	Goal setting	Project management
Presentation skills	Personality typing	Stress management
Influence skills	Customer engagement	Anger management
Communication skills	Employee engagement	Team management

Unfortunately, every company (and every trainer) knows that there's a bell curve of response to any training programme. For a given course, some people will be deeply impacted, demonstrating genuine change, with new attitudes, skills and behaviours. Others will experience little or no impact, showing no evidence of any learning having taken place. The rest will be distributed across the curve, with most people being somewhere in the middle.

Your level of clarity is the unrecognised factor that determines where on the bell curve you show up. . .

While some of this can be explained away by the fact that some people arrive with a "natural aptitude" towards a given skill set,

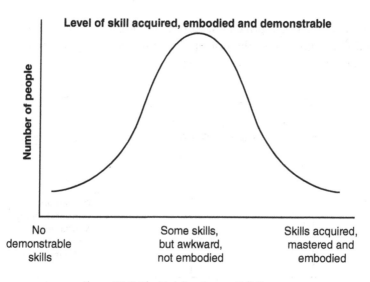

Level of skill acquired, embodied and demonstrable

Number of people

| No demonstrable skills | Some skills, but awkward, not embodied | Skills acquired, mastered and embodied |

Figure 20.2 The Training Course Bell Curve

that's only part of the story. The more important part of the story resides in the fact that a person's clarity of thought has a huge impact on their ability to learn and on their performance in the moment. All other being equal. . .

The biggest leverage point for learning any soft skill is your embodied understanding of the principles behind clarity. . .

Traditional approaches to coaching, training and organisational change are grounded in application-based learning: teaching techniques, skills and methods, then encouraging people to apply them. While these approaches can be useful for routine mechanical processes, their effectiveness drops off sharply for complex cognitive and creative skill sets. Why?

Because successful application depends on clarity and the qualities it brings.

CLARITY® training and coaching programmes are grounded in *implication-based learning*, focusing on the foundational principles that drive high performance. As individuals see the implications of these foundational principles, implementation is automatic. Insightful understanding of the principles behind clarity *literally* removes contaminated thinking and allows you to see more clearly.

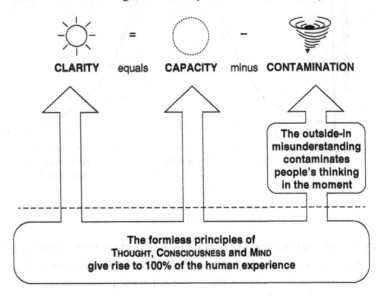

CLARITY equals **CAPACITY** minus **CONTAMINATION**

The outside-in misunderstanding contaminates people's thinking in the moment

The formless principles of THOUGHT, CONSCIOUSNESS and MIND give rise to 100% of the human experience

DISTINCTION: Information versus Implementation

It's never been easier to find high-quality **information** about how to accomplish whatever you want to accomplish. Yet it's surprising how often people struggle with **implementation**, even when they're armed with first-class tactics and a step-by-step action plan. That's because, while the intellect can always make room for some tantalising new information, it's unlikely to be implemented until it fits with the person's understanding of how life works. An update to your understanding relies on realisation.

Implementation typically involves taking responsibility, taking decisions, taking risks and taking action. These can often bring up contaminated thinking. When you can see through the mirage of that thinking, implementation is relatively straightforward. When you can't see through it, more information can look like an attractive alternative to taking action.

As you keep having realisations, and increasing your clarity of understanding, you may be surprised at how much more implementation-oriented you find yourself being.

The Secret of Successful Selling

Every successful salesperson knows that one of the most influential factors in closing a deal is the client's *experience* during the sales process. And what's the biggest factor influencing the client's experience? The experience the *salesperson* is having.

If the salesperson has a clear mind, they'll connect easily with the client, listen deeply, and respond intuitively and effectively. They'll feel secure in themselves and have a service orientation, looking for the solution that's best for the client. The client will usually pick up on the salesperson's felt experience and will bring their own clarity and comfort to the decision-making process. They may start to experience a sense of connection with one another.

But all too often, salespeople *don't* have clarity of thought; instead, their heads are clogged with contaminated thinking. They're worried about hitting their sales targets or trying to remember what the next step of their company's sales process is. They're focused on making the client like them and are afraid of feeling rejected. As a result, they come across as needy and desperate.

The solution to this is simple: clarity of understanding. When you have an insightful understanding of the principles, you know clarity is your strongest card. When your head fills up with contaminated thinking (as it does for *all* of us from time to time), you notice and allow it to self-correct. You unconsciously telegraph your sense of security, comfort and wisdom to your client as you support them in making the decision that's genuinely right for them.

Of course, this doesn't just apply to selling; it applies to all soft skills. Clarity of thought isn't just the ideal platform to *learn* from; it's also the ideal platform to *lead* from. Once again:

> *When you've got nothing on your mind,*
> *you're free to give your best.*

While there's certainly a place for skills training – I wouldn't want to be operated on by a surgeon who hadn't been to medical school – it's only part of the puzzle. I also wouldn't want to be operated on by a surgeon who had a head full of contaminated thinking about their marriage, their mortgage or their surgical skills!

So what is the leadership delusion? The misguided belief that a person can find the source of leadership *outside* themselves.

> *The true source of leadership resides in clarity, giving you*
> *what you need in the moment to deal with the matter at hand.*

While there are certainly skills to be developed and mastered, they needed to be grounded in the inner qualities of leadership. And the fastest way to develop these is by increasing your clarity of understanding. Because the symptoms are more visible than the cause, it's natural that we get seduced by the idea of working on the symptoms, looking in the direction of the attributes ("the light's better here. . ."). But it makes far more sense to nurture the cause.

> *You can nurture the cause by continuing to increase*
> *your understanding of the principles behind clarity.*

And that means that something wonderful is possible for you. . .

keep exploring ❖ connect with others
share your discoveries ❖ deepen your understanding

Thought Experiment: *What's it like for you to start recognising that you have the source of the greatest leadership capacities already right there within you?*

What the Research Says: In her article, "The Modern Education System Was Designed to Teach Future Factory Workers to be 'Punctual, Docile, and Sober,'" reporter Allison Schrager describes the role of factory schools in producing a compliant workforce during the Industrial Revolution. Industrialists saw a need for "social conditioning" if labourers were to transition from domestic and farm work to the factory setting. The Prussian model of factory-style schools was widely adopted and has been used ever since. Unfortunately, many of the implicit "social lessons" it was designed to impart (e.g. follow orders, don't question authority) are no longer fit for purpose in the Information Revolution.

> Schrager, A. (2018). The modern education system was designed to teach future factory workers to be "punctual, docile, and sober." *Yahoo!news*, June 29.

You can read the article at www.JamieSmart.com/research/Clarity20

Additional Resources

www.JamieSmart.com/Clarity20

21

Living a Life You Love

....

"We must be willing to get rid of the life we've planned, so as to have the life that is waiting for us. The old skin has to be shed before the new one can come."

Joseph Campbell
Mythologist, writer and lecturer

"Now let me ask you something I think we all know the answer to: The test is rigged, isn't it? You programmed it to be unwinnable. . ."

In a pivotal scene from the film *Star Trek*, a young James T Kirk (played by Chris Pine) is defending himself against the charge of cheating on the Kobayashi Maru test (a highly realistic battle simulation designed to gauge the trainee's response to a no-win scenario). Kirk is the first person ever to beat the test, but Spock (the test's designer) has accused him of breaking the rules. Kirk's defence is that *the test itself* is a cheat; that if a game has been designed to be unwinnable, you don't have to play by the rules of the game.

So how is this relevant?

Here's how: The outside-in misunderstanding turns *life* into an unwinnable game. The *"I'll be happy when. . ."* and *"I couldn't be happy if. . ."* superstitions promise us that happiness, security and well-being are waiting for us "out there" in the distance or in the future. Whether it's five years, five miles or five seconds away, the outside-in misunderstanding tells us that our heart's desire is just out of reach, just out there at the end of our thinking. But it's not true and it never has been. That's not how it works.

When we look to the world of form for our happiness, security and peace of mind, we're looking in the wrong direction. It doesn't matter whether it's the "there" of material possessions or personal accomplishments, self-improvement or spirituality. The moment we think there's somewhere to get to, and that there is better than here, we've stepped out of our sanity and into an unwinnable game.

So what does it mean to step out of the unwinnable game and back into our sanity? What does it mean to live a life you love, regardless of its ups and downs?

The Search Is Over

Early in my career as a trainer and coach, but before I'd been introduced to the principles behind clarity, I used to run a workshop called "The Art of Being." At the start of the first day, as people began to get comfortable, I would say something like this:

You know that thing that you've been searching for. . . your heart's desire? The thing you've been seeking for all these years? I invite you to open to the possibility that you can have it today. . . Have it here. . . Have it now. . .

The moment they heard this, people would start shifting uncomfortably in their seats, and I would mimic their internal dialogue, anxiously saying:

I know what you're thinking. . . you're thinking, "I really do want it. . . And I'm really looking forward to having it. . . But today's a bit soon. . . See, I've got a busy month, and rather a lot on my mind. . . But I was thinking, a few weeks from now is looking really good. . . It's what I want most in the world, so I'll definitely make space for it. . . But if you could just arrange things so it arrives next month. . . That'll give me time to do what I need to do. . . Next month will be just perfect. . ."

Whether you call it the self-image, the ego or contaminated thinking, there's one thing it can't stand: the knowledge that the life you desire is *already here*, that you don't need anything else for you to be OK, that you can live a life you love, starting *now*. Of course, I understood that *intellectually* in those days, but I didn't have an embodied understanding of it. So I kept on seeking. Kept on searching. Until one day I realised something for myself. . .

The search is over.

As you continue deepening your understanding of the principles behind clarity, you'll see that searching and seeking is inconsistent with the knowledge that you already have everything you need within you, that searching and seeking is just another flavour of the unwinnable game. The very feeling we've been interpreting as "there's something I need to search for" is, in fact, the feeling of contaminated thinking, and nothing else. There's nothing missing. You were born whole, and you still are whole.

The moment we stop looking outside ourselves for that which can only be found within, our whole world changes. As your world-view continues shifting from outside-in to inside-out, it's inevitable that you'll love yourself and your life more and more, *whatever* form it takes.

Reality Check

Am I saying that understanding these principles will transform the *circumstances* of a person's life into something wonderful? No. I'm saying that when a person sees life from a greater clarity of understanding, they have a deeper, more profound experience of life, *whatever* their circumstances.

Of course, when a person is living in a richer felt experience, and allowing themselves to be guided by wisdom, the circumstances of their lives often change, too, but there's the paradox:

Once you realise your happiness, security and well-being isn't dependent on your circumstances, It can be easier to change your circumstances.

A practical example

Two people doing the same kind of work are both applying for the same position. Both are equally well qualified for the new post. The only difference between the two is that one has an embodied understanding of the principles behind clarity and the other doesn't. When they go to the job interview, the contrast is huge. One is clear-headed, relaxed and alert, while the other is feeling anxious and insecure. One listens deeply to the interviewer and starts feeling connected to them, while the other feels self-conscious and isolated. One is in touch with innate wisdom and creativity, while the other has a congested, speedy mind. Who do you think is more likely to get the job? The person who feels peaceful, present and secure in themselves? Or the one who's feeling anxious, insecure and needy?

Life seems to respond in a similar way. When you're living from clarity, being guided by wisdom, life is free to unfold gracefully with each step you take. There will still be ups and downs; that's part of being human. But we've evolved to appreciate life. Our psychological immune system exists to guide us into a natural, enjoyable experience of life. Our natural response to life is gratitude and appreciation, when there's nothing else in the way. And what gets in the way? Contaminated thinking!

What follows is a list of gentle reminders to help you stay on track, living a life you love. They are not rules or how-tos, but they may serve to spark an insight or an a-ha that makes a difference for you at one time or another.

More important, they are not something you need to do, practice or even remember. Everything you need is already right there within you; there's nothing you need to do to have a life you love.

Appreciation

When you find yourself in a more profound felt experience of life, enjoy it. This isn't a doing – it's more of a not doing. Our deeper feelings of love, peace and well-being carry valuable information that can correct our thought system, bringing it into closer connection with reality. So when you notice these feelings arising, allow yourself to stay with them.

Gratitude

Gratitude is like fertiliser for new realisations. When you're feeling grateful for what you've already realised, you create fertile soil for fresh insights to blossom. Conversely, searching and seeking (with the sense of lack they imply) is like soaking the ground in weed-killer. Gratitude and appreciation are natural responses to insight, and to being alive, so you can enjoy them when they come.

Ease off on trying to figure it out

Like the sun behind the clouds, clarity, security and peace of mind are always within you, whether you're aware of it or not. But you can't *think* your way to clarity and well-being, so there's no point in trying to figure it out. That just creates more thinking, which is the only thing that ever blocks a person's awareness of clarity in the first place. Instead, you can relax, and recognise that *everything* you're experiencing is a demonstration of the principles in action.

Understanding is a rational goal

Everyone likes to feel good, but when we make that our goal, we tend to use our old habits of thinking to achieve it (with predictable results). When your goal is increasing your clarity of understanding, every experience becomes an opportunity to learn, to see how the principles behind clarity are creating an experience of life in this moment.

Pause when agitated

When you're feeling anxious, insecure or agitated, your thinking seems absolutely real. But we're always living in the experience of THOUGHT, and an agitated feeling is letting us know the kind of THOUGHT-generated perceptual reality we're currently in – nothing more, nothing less. While I don't recommend you *do* anything about it – let it change when it changes – wisdom will insightfully remind you where your experience is *actually* coming from. That's the signal that the system is self-correcting. When you realise that (or even catch the barest glimpse of it), pay attention, and it will guide you back to clarity.

Look to the source

In any situation, we're either aligned with the outside-in misunderstanding (looking towards the *products* of MIND, THOUGHT and CONSCIOUSNESS) or with the inside-out reality (looking towards the formless source, the principles themselves). When we're lost in contaminated thinking, it can seem like it's the *only* way of perceiving a situation. But, in any moment, you can look away from that perception and towards its source. Once again, this isn't a doing, but rather something that happens automatically when you step out of the unwinnable game, and keep waking up to the source of wisdom and realisation you have within.

You don't need to be vigilant

So many people (myself included) have learned to be vigilant with their thinking, trying to monitor and manage their experience.

This results in a bunch more thinking, which can block them from the experience of clarity, which is the very thing they were trying to get in the *first* place. You don't need to do this anymore. When you have a realisation, it updates your thought system. You don't need to work on it.

Be kind to yourself

If being hard on yourself was going to work, it would have worked by now. I encourage you to be kind, gentle and loving with yourself. We all have flaws, frailties and weaknesses; you can love yourself as you are, warts and all. Paradoxically, when we love and accept ourselves as we are, things that used to be utterly resistant to change can suddenly shift effortlessly. Or not. Be kind to yourself, either way. Once again, this isn't really something to do; it's more something to be aware of and open to. As contaminated thinking continues falling away, you may start noticing just how much you already love yourself, but just hadn't fully realised it until now. (If that sentence makes you feel uncomfortable, you might like to ask yourself, honestly, *"Where do I believe my experience is coming from, right now?"* We're living in the feeling Thought in every single moment, including this one!)

Lighten up

Oscar Wilde famously said *"Life is too important to be taken seriously."* The feeling of seriousness is a signal letting us know about the virtual reality goggles we're currently wearing, but when we don't know that, it can be a grind. While there are situations that require a serious response, it's not mandatory to *feel* serious about it. Love, peace and clarity often carry the information you need to solve the more challenging issues in life, and those deeper feelings are incompatible with the *feeling* of seriousness (though it's still fine to behave seriously when necessary).

Allow wisdom to guide you

Sydney Banks once said of MIND, CONSCIOUSNESS and THOUGHT, *"If you have enough faith that those three principles – left alone – will guide you through life, they'll take you from the most deplorable conditions to happiness. No matter what."* Given the chance, wisdom will guide you from wherever you are now to your most fulfilling, inspiring life. Wisdom doesn't make us immune to the ups and downs of life, but it helps us to live life in a way that fits perfectly with who we are. As you learn to navigate by wisdom, and deepen your understanding of the principles behind clarity, you'll find yourself living a life you love, more and more each day.

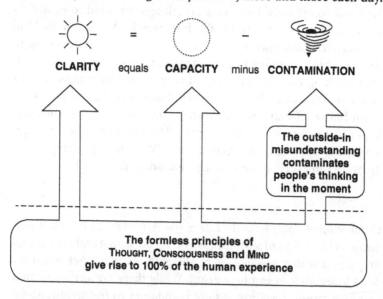

CLARITY equals **CAPACITY** minus **CONTAMINATION**

The outside-in misunderstanding contaminates people's thinking in the moment

The formless principles of THOUGHT, CONSCIOUSNESS and MIND give rise to 100% of the human experience

The power of principles revisited

Earlier in the book, I used the metaphor of a football being held underwater to symbolise innate clarity, resilience and well-being. As soon as the hand holding the football releases it, the ball rises to the surface.

The reason the ball rises so reliably is because of buoyancy. When you immerse a floating object in a container of water, the pressure increases the deeper you go due to the weight of the water above. The differences in water pressure exert an upward force on the immersed object, which raises it to the surface. There are precise factors that govern the rate at which a submerged object will rise, including weight, density and friction. But these factors are all governed by *a single factor*: the universal principle of gravity. As previously mentioned, a principle is "the fundamental source or basis for something."

Buoyancy works the same way for everyone on the planet because gravity doesn't play favourites. It's nothing personal, and there are no exceptions. In the same way, the principles that give rise to innate clarity, resilience and well-being work the same way for everyone on the planet. It's nothing personal, and there are no exceptions.

So, if this is genuinely a "new paradigm," what does that mean for the world of business and work in the years to come? And what does it mean for us as individuals?

---

keep exploring ⁃⁝⁃ connect with others
share your discoveries ⁃⁝⁃ deepen your understanding

Thought Experiment: *Have you already started to notice that any lingering sense you may have had that there's somewhere to get to (and that there is better than here) was an illusion? That the search is over?*

What the Research Says: Here's an excerpt from my book *RESULTS* (©2016 Jamie Smart):

High performance leads to superb results
People give their best performances when they've got nothing on their mind. When your mind is clear, you're available to the moment, connected to your innate source of guidance, resilience and creativity. And where does high performance come from? Your state of mind.

How your state of mind affects your performance

In their December 2014 Harvard Business Review article, 'How Your State of Mind Affects Your Performance', researchers Caillet, Hirshberg and Petti reported their findings from a survey of 740 leaders internationally. 94% of the leaders identified the states that drove the highest levels of performance as 'calm', 'happy' and 'energized' (CHE). At the other end of the spectrum, leaders admitted to spending a certain amount of time in low-performance states; 'frustrated', 'anxious', 'tired' and 'stressed' (FATS). The article suggested that CHE states not only drove high performance; these states also seemed to be 'transmitted' to other people. Conversely, the FATS states often delivered short-term results, but were damaging in the long term, particularly in the domain of relationships.

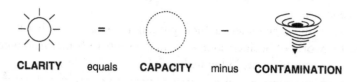

CLARITY   equals   **CAPACITY**   minus   **CONTAMINATION**

When we struggle with FATS states, we've been hijacked by contaminated thinking. The CHE states, on the other hand, are natural for us when our minds are free from contaminated thinking.

You can use the CLARITY Impact Elevator overleaf to get a sense of which states of mind you've been spending time in. An increase in your clarity of understanding can lead to a jump in your state of mind 'baseline', with a knock-on improvement in your performance and well-being.

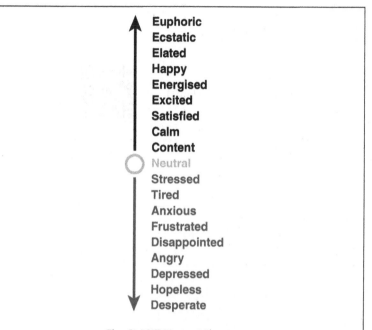

The CLARITY Impact Elevator

Caillet, A. Hursberg, J., & Petti, S. (2014). How your state of mind affects your performance. Harvard Business Review (8 December).

You can get the HBR article here:
www.JamieSmart.com/research/Clarity21

Additional Resources

www.JamieSmart.com/Clarity21

22

Capitalising on Chaos, Complexity and Uncertainty

....

"We are at that very point in time when a 400-year-old age is dying and another is struggling to be born – a shifting of culture, science, society and institutions enormously greater than the world has ever experienced."

Dee Ward Hock
Founder and former CEO of Visa

"Everything that can be invented has been invented. . ."

A popular myth credits the 1899 commissioner of the US patent office with this quaintly absurd statement. And while there's no *hard* evidence that he actually said it, the last 100 years have been peppered with short-sighted predictions asserting what wouldn't be useful, wouldn't be feasible or wouldn't be possible. All the way from the first telephone to the world wide web, as each technological revolution is on the verge of dawning, someone goes on record to say it's not going to happen. Then it happens.

The world is changing fast. Increases in speed, complexity and knowledge are accompanied by attention poverty, time scarcity and information overwhelm. People shake their heads in the face of chaos, complexity and uncertainty, harking back to simpler times. But what if there's a larger pattern behind the changes we're experiencing?

The Waves of Transformation

In their seminal book *The Third Wave*, Alvin and Heidi Toffler use the metaphor of waves to describe the revolutionary changes that have swept over the globe throughout history. Each wave solves existing problems, while creating new possibilities, benefits and challenges. Solutions to the new problems are delivered by the next wave. In brief, here are the three waves the Tofflers described:

First wave: The Agricultural Revolution (domestication)
The first wave starts around 8000 BC with the *domestication and farming* of plants and animals, resulting in stabilisation of food supplies. Over time, increasing *agricultural wealth* allows farming cultures with *food economies* to dominate hunter-gatherer cultures.

Second wave: The Industrial Revolution (mechanisation)
The second wave starts around 1760 with the *mechanisation* of manual labour, resulting in the mass production of goods. *Industrial wealth* results in *manufacturing economies* that dominate agricultural societies.

Third wave: The Information Revolution (digitisation)
The third wave starts around 1940 with the *digitisation* of information. The *knowledge economy* rewards *informational wealth* and dominates information-poor industrial cultures.

The current wave shift

There are numerous signals that let us know the third wave (Information Revolution) is continuing to grow and the second wave (Industrial Revolution) is ebbing. In fact, the attention poverty, time scarcity, information saturation and connection starvation so many people are experiencing is the inevitable consequence of the outside-in misunderstanding in the context of the current wave shift.

The uncertainties and complexities we face are too great to be solved by intellect and analysis alone. Clarity (with all it entails) is the key to solving the big issues that face us, and to creating a sustainable future for ourselves, for our organisations and for the generations that follow us. . .

- We need *clarity*, so we can bring a systemic perspective to solving problems and creating possibilities.
- We need *direction*, so we can create a meaningful and compelling future.
- We need *wisdom*, so we can make prudent decisions in the face of chaos and complexity.
- We need *connection*, so we can enjoy the richness and sense of belonging it brings.
- We need *authenticity*, so we can be true to ourselves and lead with integrity.
- We need *resilience*, so we can negotiate life's many challenges, with grace and dignity.
- We need *creativity*, so we can create the sustainable solutions and innovations we require.
- We need *presence*, so we can inspire trust and stay connected with reality.

As each wave emerges, the culture embraces new stories about its future, new images of itself (remember those 1950s newsreels predicting the robot-enabled, leisure-age of the future?). As the previous wave's future images start to fade and disintegrate, positive new stories are needed that align with the new wave and nourish the culture with hope for what it promises.

This is one of the key tasks for leaders: to create inspiring and compelling visions of our possible futures.

There are early indicators (and early adopters) as each wave emerges. For instance, computers used to be the domain of scientists, the military and big business. As the third wave gathered power, "computer geeks," hobbyists and other early adopters got involved. The past 30 years have seen computers move from the specialist fringe to the consumer mainstream as they've become integrated into our daily lives.

This last point is essential. There's a close correlation between adoption of emergent wave drivers (*domestication, mechanisation, digitisation*) and commercial success. The individuals and companies that embraced the Industrial Revolution prospered. The early adopters of information technology won a massive advantage over those who hesitated. In fact, the largest and most profitable enterprises are those that fully embrace the emergent wave drivers (early third wave examples include Apple, Microsoft, Google, Amazon, etc.).

We're now in the midst of the Information Revolution – more people than ever before earn their living participating in knowledge work. So what's going to start transforming the knowledge economy?

Early signs of the fourth wave

The advance signals of the fourth wave started arriving in the late nineteenth century with the birth of the field of psychology. The business world was quick to embrace psychology for commercial purposes, using it to influence public opinion, customers and employees alike. Over the past 40 years, the signals have been arriving more and more quickly:

- The rise of the human potential movement, positive psychology and increasing interest in personal development
- Identification of the need for "emotional intelligence" in the workplace
- The desire for authenticity, integrity and transparency in the companies we do business with

- Increasing business focus on identifying and developing the qualities of leadership
- The decline of many institutions that we previously relied on for a sense of security, purpose and belonging (e.g. religion, education system, postal service, civil service, large companies, jobs for life, etc.)
- People looking elsewhere for security, belonging and purpose as they pursue "portfolio careers" and move towards greater independence and personal freedom

Understanding the nature of Thought

The first, second and third waves have each been driven by an insightful understanding of the wave's key leverage point:

- First wave (Agricultural Revolution): understanding of *farming/ agriculture*
- Second wave (Industrial Revolution): understanding of *mechanisation/industry*
- Third wave (Information Revolution): understanding of *information/digitisation/computerisation*

The deeper our understanding of the leverage point within a given wave, the more power we have to create value.

Most people these days would concede that their thinking has at least *some* part to play in their experience of life. The advance signals of the fourth wave have seen people try to influence their thinking in a variety of ways, using techniques, rituals and methodologies. As people start to see that thinking plays a role in their experience, it's natural that they would try and use it to *influence* that experience. But while people have correctly identified that thinking is an incredibly powerful leverage point, the real power comes from understanding the nature of Thought.

- Fourth wave (Thought revolution): understanding of the nature of *Thought*

The experience economy

There are already numerous signs that we're moving towards an experience economy. As people become more time poor, attention starved and values focused, the quality of their *experience* of life becomes more important. People are seeking out pockets of experience, like oases in a desert.

- Starbucks has built a multibillion-dollar business based on encouraging people to carve 20–30 minutes out of an already busy day so they can sit on a sofa drinking an expensive coffee with their name written on the cup. A 20–30 minute *experience*, repeated daily for millions of people.
- The Apple Store has helped turn Apple into the most profitable company in the world by creating a brilliantly executed in-store *experience* and introducing people to exquisitely designed, high-utility "lifestyle products."
- Adventure tourism (adrenalin sports experiences), sacred travel (spiritual hotspots for New Agers), extreme tourism (travel to very dangerous places) and eco-tourism (ecologically friendly travel) are all examples of people's willingness to pay for values-based *experiences*.

So how does an individual or a business capitalise on the chaos, complexity and uncertainty that the current wave-shift is bringing?

The critical fourth-wave factor

There's one thing that affects the quality of *experience* a person has more than any other factor: your level of clarity, the state of mind you're in when you're having the experience. Clarity is "the difference that makes the difference" when it comes to any experience:

- A couple go to a movie. One of them is fully engaged and loves it (clarity), the other is bored and distracted (contaminated thinking).

- Six people are sitting in a business meeting. The difference between a grindingly dull waste of time and a productive, generative experience is the clarity of the participants.
- A family of five go on holiday. Four of them love it, but the teenage son finds it tedious. Clarity is what makes the difference.

The value of an event is dependent on the quality of the experience the person has. The quality of the experience a person has is 100% dependent on their level of clarity when they're having the experience. This is why understanding the nature of THOUGHT is so fundamental to the experience economy.

As the Information Revolution continues to gobble up people's attention, the critical factor influencing their ability to enjoy any given experience will be clarity.

So far, in the experience economy, businesses have taken responsibility for managing more and more of the external aspects of a person's experience. Video game designers have taken it a step further and have become masters of influencing the neural events that their players experience.

Some people argue that the next step isn't the experience economy, that we're now in the "connection economy" or the "creativity economy." They may be correct, and whether they are or not, the leverage points are still the same: clarity of thought and clarity of understanding. The THOUGHT revolution is already in progress.

The future belongs to those who are willing to go one step further than that, and start influencing their staff and customers' understanding of how life works.

Reality Check

"But wait!" I hear you say. "If everyone's walking around feeling fulfilled and clear-headed, won't it be like living in a society of zombie bliss robots? What about my personality, my individuality, my self?"

There's nothing to worry about. The person who is living from the outside-in misunderstanding is far more robotic (innocently) than a person living from clarity and well-being. As your clarity of understanding continues increasing, you're far more likely to be courageous, take challenging decisions and be guided by wisdom.

The reality of the inside-out nature of life has the power to touch our true identity, our essence, our spirits. And as we continue waking up to our true nature, we discover the very thing that can make the biggest difference in our own lives also represents our most profound contribution to humanity, the world and to all of life. . .

keep exploring ⬦ connect with others
share your discoveries ⬦ deepen your understanding

Thought Experiment: *The Industrial Revolution gave rise to a massive, sustained increase in the standard of living for huge numbers of people. This was a step change unlike anything in humanity's history. Has it occurred to you that we could be on the verge of another, similarly profound step change?*

What the Research Says: *The Third Wave* is Heidi and Alvin Toffler's seminal work describing the waves of transformation that have swept the planet over the past 10,000 years. The Calculemus.org summary/lecture notes on the book are excellent and have been cited over 16,000 times.

The Toffler's book was published over 40 years ago, but they were able to sense the tectonic shifts society was going to be undergoing:

Humanity faces a quantum leap forward. It faces the deepest social upheaval and creative restructuring of all time. Without clearly recognizing it, we are engaged in building a remarkable new civilization from the ground up. . . What is happening now is nothing less than a global revolution, a quantum jump in history.

You can find the summary at www.JamieSmart.com/research/Clarity22

Additional Resources

www.JamieSmart.com/Clarity22

23

The Art of Sustainable Change

....

"Culture eats strategy for breakfast."

Peter Drucker
Management consultant and writer

"We have developed speed but we have shut ourselves in. Machinery that gives abundance has left us in want. Our knowledge has made us cynical, our cleverness hard and unkind. We think too much and feel too little. More than machinery we need humanity. More than cleverness we need kindness. . ."

Charlie Chaplin's arrestingly beautiful final speech from *The Great Dictator* (1940) seems more relevant today than ever, echoing across the intervening years like a prophesy.

Artists like Chaplin are the canaries in humanity's coal mine, sensing our emerging patterns and potentials long before they become obvious to everyone else. And, while his warnings about our relationship to technology are uncannily prescient, his message of hope for our individual and collective future shines through even more strongly.

The End of the Caterpillar's World

Once a caterpillar sheds its skin to reveal the chrysalis that will offer protection during the process of metamorphosis, the caterpillar starts to disintegrate, resulting in a kind of "caterpillar soup." This creative broth contains a small number of surviving body parts as well as a huge number of imaginal cells that have been contained within the body of the caterpillar since it was born. The imaginal cells start to join up, and the butterfly emerges from the caterpillar soup.

This metamorphosis from caterpillar to butterfly can be a compelling metaphor for personal and collective transformation. . .

- The blueprint of the butterfly already exists within the body of the caterpillar, contained in the imaginal cells. Similarly, the pattern of your transformation is already there within you, contained within the formless energy of who you really are.

- The caterpillar doesn't work at becoming a butterfly; it transforms in harmony with its pre-existing nature. Similarly, you don't have to struggle or work at transformation. Aligning to who you really are is in harmony with your pre-existing nature.

- The change from caterpillar to butterfly is a metamorphosis, a genuine transformation at the most fundamental level. Similarly, aligning to your most inspired and inspiring life is a genuine transformation, a profound reordering of your experience of life and how you relate to it.

The implicit ability to understand the true nature of life is there within each one of us, like the imaginal cells in the body of the caterpillar. As we start waking up to that deeper nature, our experience of life is transformed, and we start to live in a new world.

Paradoxically, as we increase our clarity of understanding, the external form life takes is often optimised in ways we never would have predicted from within our old, outside-in misunderstanding. Whatever form it takes, there's a growing sense that you're living a life that fits you perfectly.

A deeper, more profound understanding of life also gives you new eyes. Situations that were once complex and baffling suddenly look much simpler when you can see the principles of THOUGHT, CONSCIOUSNESS and MIND playing out. Problems that seemed impossible to solve often melt away when clarity and wisdom come into play. Frustration can be transformed to understanding, and resentment to compassion as we see that every person is subject to the ups and downs of life and that these principles are creating a unique, individual experience of reality for each of us.

Separate realities

Once we realise our experience of life is being created from the inside-out, it follows that we each live in a unique, THOUGHT-generated experiential reality. No two people live in the same experience of reality, and each person's reality seems *real* to them (remember: THOUGHT creates the world then says *"I didn't do it."*).

Almost everyone on the planet today is operating from within the outside-in misunderstanding; very few of us realise the fact of separate realities. Even when we insightfully understand the inside-out nature of life, it's still surprising how often we get tricked into believing we live in an outside-in world.

But as you continue increasing your clarity of understanding, you become more and more likely to see the psychological innocence in yourself and others. Every person is doing what makes sense to them at their current level of understanding. If we had their embodied understanding of life, we'd be doing the same thing they are. When our clarity of understanding rises, we act accordingly. As we see more clearly and feel better, we start to do better.

> ## Reality Check
>
> *"What about murderous criminals and tyrannical dictators?"* I hear you ask. *"Are you honestly suggesting they're innocent, that they're not responsible for their crimes?"* Of course they're responsible for the crimes they've committed, and they need to be dealt with accordingly. But they are *psychologically* innocent. As strange as it seems, their misdeeds "made sense" to them from the THOUGHT-generated experiential reality they were living in at the time, misinformed and compounded by the outside-in misunderstanding.
>
> In Semmelweis's day, doctors innocently infected patients with dirty scalpels. It was an inevitable result of their level of understanding at the time. As soon as they had a deeper understanding of the nature of germs, they acted accordingly, washing their hands and sterilising their instruments.

Most of humanity's problems at the individual, organisational and global scale are the inevitable result of our current level of (mis)understanding. As we get a deeper understanding individually and collectively, we'll act accordingly. As more and more people start seeing through the outside-in misunderstanding, our world will change.

The network effect

Metcalfe's law (aka the *network effect*) describes the impact that one additional user has on the value of a network to all the other users. When only one person had a telephone, it had no value, but as each user was added, the value of the service increased for everyone. The same is true for email, Twitter, Bitcoin and all other services that have a networked aspect. As each person is added to the network, the value of the network increases for everyone.

With a metaphorical leap, you can look at superstitions and new paradigms in a similar way. Today, the vast majority of humanity is operating from the outside-in misunderstanding. By the time a child is six years old, they've been told in 100,000 different ways that they live in an outside-in world.

In a world where outside-in is a "fact" for almost everyone, the network effect is strong; the outside-in misunderstanding is reinforced wherever we look.

But when you wake up to the inside-out nature of reality, two things happen: the strength of the outside-in network effect reduces and the strength of the inside-out network effect increases. As you wake up to the inside-out nature of life, you make the power of the inside-out understanding stronger for everyone, as well as making it easier for the next person to see it for themselves.

Thought Experiment

London's Wembley stadium holds a staggering 90,000 people. Imagine it, filled to capacity, with each person holding an unlit candle in their hand. Suddenly the lights go out, and the stadium is plunged into darkness. In the midst of the blackout, a single candle is lit. Everyone can see the tiny pinprick of light, and they watch as the light touches the candles of the people standing near it. Those candles flare into life. Now there are 10 candles burning, then 50, then 100! The amount of light from the candles increases, and now you can make out people's faces. Within minutes, 10,000 candles are burning, and light fills the stadium. Then 20,000, then 30,000, and so on. . .

The moment your candle starts burning, you increase the amount of light available for everyone, and the darkness is further diminished.

The world is changing more rapidly than ever before; old systems are crumbling as new ones emerge to take their place. And while there are more people on the planet than at any point in history, we live at a time when each individual has enormous power to take part in creating our world.

Management guru Peter Drucker famously said that "culture eats strategy for breakfast." Disruptive organisations demonstrate the truth of Drucker's assertion. He was implicitly acknowledging that even the most brilliant strategy is reliant on *people* to implement it; people whose culture (the shared set of stories, values, beliefs, assumptions, understandings and worldviews they live from) means the difference between success and failure.

In her book *Conscious Evolution*, futurist Barbara Marx Hubbard used the term *cultural creatives* to describe people who are transforming and waking up to their true nature. Hubbard took the butterfly metaphor one step further, suggesting that cultural creatives are the imaginal cells in the caterpillar of our civilisation, coming together to form the butterfly of our collective future.

If this seems far-fetched, ask yourself this: What would your company, organisation or community be like if everyone in it had an insightful understanding of the principles behind clarity? What would your world be like if everyone you knew had an insightful understanding of the inside-out nature of life? How would they behave if they already felt good in themselves and about themselves? How would they act if they were guided more by wisdom than by contaminated thinking? I encourage you to imagine for yourself what our world would look like from this new paradigm.

The job of creating a coherent vision for the future of humanity is far beyond the scope of this book. But, while we have some massive challenges facing us, we have good reason to be hopeful. . .

- Most people on the planet have never been directly involved in a war.
- Medical science is able to treat more conditions than at any time in history.
- Customers are calling for the companies that serve them to be increasingly authentic, transparent and socially responsible.
- Citizens are demanding that the environment be placed on government and corporate agendas.
- Global connectivity means that new ideas spread faster, more effectively and more easily than at any point in history.

It's understandable that people sometimes feel powerless and overwhelmed when confronting the big problems and challenges that face humanity. But there's an even bigger reason to be optimistic. You see, there's an incredible elegance implicit in the truth behind our experience of life. The outside-in misunderstanding means that people are *innocently* looking outside themselves for something that can only ever come from within.

Remember the table from Chapter 4? The formless principles of MIND, THOUGHT and CONSCIOUSNESS are the "inside" I'm referring to when I say your experience is being created "from the inside out." These three principles are "inside"; everything else is "outside."

Inside	Outside
The formless principles of. . .	Everything else including. . .
● MIND ● THOUGHT ● CONSCIOUSNESS (your true identity)	● Time, space and matter ● Personality/self-image/self-concept ● Beliefs, thoughts and concepts ● Physical bodies ● Current circumstances ● Past and future ● Feelings and emotions

It doesn't work outside-in; it only works inside-out. And when we truly see that for ourselves, we resonate with it; we are touched by it. Stop and consider this for a moment. . .

Just as the blueprint of your most inspiring, successful life already exists within the consciousness at the heart of your being, the blueprint of humanity's most inspiring, successful possibility exists within our collective consciousness. . .

I've always loved this statement from the priest, scientist and philosopher Teilhard de Chardin: "We are not human beings having a spiritual experience. We are spiritual beings having a human experience." I've taken the liberty of adapting it, as follows:

We are not human beings having a spiritual experience. We are one spiritual being having eight billion human experiences. And who you really are is that one spiritual being.

Who you really are is CONSCIOUSNESS itself.

Your response to the desire for genuine transformation boils down to a simple decision. Do you choose to. . .

1. Play an unwinnable game, struggling within the outside-in misunderstanding, or. . .
2. Focus on increasing your clarity of understanding, aligning with your true nature and living your most inspiring, fulfilling and successful life.

It's worth taking some time to reflect on this choice. Contaminated thinking can be compelling, and we all get tricked by it from time to time, but it's just an illusion. When you decide to make it a priority to deepen your understanding of the principles behind clarity, you're aligning yourself more closely with reality and with your true nature.

This is the essence of clarity.

We are all in this together, each playing our part in the unfolding of life, our personal and collective evolution. The fact that you're reading this book means that you're looking in the right direction: at the principles that are creating our experience of life. Keep looking in this direction, and your clarity of understanding will continue increasing as you enjoy the powerful benefits of insight and realisation.

Above all, remember this: We're all human; we each have our ups and downs. Our experience of reality is being created from the inside-out, using the principles of MIND, CONSCIOUSNESS and THOUGHT. And while we don't get to choose the timescale, new realisations can show up in any moment. And when fresh realisations arrive, our world changes.

keep exploring ⊹ connect with others
share your discoveries ⊹ deepen your understanding

Thought Experiment: *What if there's a bigger picture here? Many forward-thinking leaders believe that we're in the midst of a profound societal transformation. Could the fact that you're reading this book mean that you're an integral part of the societal DNA for what's to come?*

What the Research Says: Researchers Zhang, Liu and Xu published an article in the *Journal of Computer Science and Technology* called "Tencent and Facebook Data Validate Metcalfe's Law." Metcalfe's law states that the value of a network is proportional to the square of the number of nodes in the network. For example, when only 10 people had phones, the notional value of the network was 100 (10 × 10). Once 1000 people had phones, the notional value of the phone network was 1,000,000 (1000 × 1000). The researchers were able to validate the law using data from the companies Facebook and Tencent. While Metcalfe's law is typically referenced in relation to technology adoption, it also reveals something deeper about the human beings using those technologies. As such, it's an interesting metaphor for the adoption of a first principles understanding of human psychology.

Zhang, X. Z., Liu, J. J., & Xu, Z. W. (2015). Tencent and Facebook data validate Metcalfe's law. Computer Science and Technology, 30, 246–251.

You can read the article at www.JamieSmart.com/research/Clarity23

Additional Resources

www.JamieSmart.com/Clarity23

24

Inspired Action

"Run from what's comfortable. Forget safety. Live where you fear to live. Destroy your reputation. Be notorious. I have tried prudent planning long enough. From now on I'll be mad."

Rumi
Poet

"Inspiration often shows up when you're already doing something else, so. . ."

Show up. . .

Get in the game. . .

Stay in the game. . .

Step into the unknown. . .

And keep experimenting. . .

Pause and reflect from time to time. . .

Discover your "how" as you take the next step. . .

Remember, you're living in the feeling of your thinking. . .

When your wisdom reminds you of this, relax. . .
The system is self-correcting. . .

If you find you're pointed in the wrong direction,
adjust as necessary. . .

Become willing to make mistakes and learn from them. . .

Keep increasing your clarity of understanding. . .

You're capable of far more than you think. . .

Because you are far more than you think. . .

Discover your path by walking it. . .

And be grateful for the highs. . .

Graceful in the lows. . .

And do your best. . .

To enjoy yourself. . .

Every step of the way. . .

Secure in your increasing understanding. . .

Of how the system works. . .

> ### keep exploring ✛ connect with others
> ### share your discoveries ✛ deepen your understanding
>
> **Thought Experiment:** *Enough reflection; it's time for some action. When you get to the additional resources for this chapter, you'll find a version of the preceding page that you can print out and put up on your wall. There's lots of other good stuff there for you too, as your reward for making it all the way to the end of this book. Thanks for reading this book; I look forward to connecting with you in person or online at some point in the future.*
>
> **What the Research Says:** At the heart of this book is the assertion that the source of resilience, realisation and transformation resides within you, at the heart of your being. In Chapter 2, we referred to the States of Consciousness Questionnaire (SOCQ) used by consciousness researchers as a measure of mystical experiences. One of the qualities measured by the SOCQ is the "noetic quality," described by the psychologist William James as follows:
>
> *. . . mystical states seem to those who experience them to be also states of knowledge. They are states of insight into the depths of truth unplumbed by the discursive intellect. They are illuminations, revelations, full of significance and importance, all inarticulate though they remain; and as a rule they carry with them a curious sense of authority for after-time.*
>
> While we will continue to see research published which illuminates the principles behind clarity, the "research" that will make the biggest difference in *your* life will be the insights you realise for yourself. Furthermore, when it comes to sharing this understanding with others, it will be your own realisations that will carry the greatest authority.

Additional Resources

www.JamieSmart.com/Clarity24

25

Troubleshooting Enlightenment

....

"The mind is its own place, and in itself can make a heaven of hell, a hell of heaven..."

John Milton
Poet

"My main hope is eventually, in modern education field, introduce education about warm-heartedness, not based on religion, but based on common experience and a common sort of sense, and then scientific finding."

The Dalai Lama was being interviewed upon receiving the Templeton Prize (awarded annually to a living person who advances Sir John Templeton's vision: "harnessing the power of the sciences to explore the deepest questions of the universe and humankind's place and purpose within it").

As the Dalai Lama shared his hope for the future, he revealed his intuitive sense that science would eventually uncover a source of mental health and well-being common to us all. It is my assertion that the principles behind clarity represent this source.

In this chapter, we're going to look at some common challenges and issues people grapple with through the lens of this new paradigm. With this in mind, it's worth knowing the following:

- You have good reason to be hopeful. No matter what you've been through or are up against, there is a source of resilience, realisation and transformation residing at the heart of your being.
- That source is the solution to all the challenges listed here. That source is within you and can provide the guidance and solutions you need.

While this chapter may prove useful and insightful for practitioners and members of the public alike, it is not a substitute for working with a skilled coach, therapist or physician (ideally one with a deep understanding of the principles we're exploring here).

All the transformations in the case studies that follow happened as a result of people having realisations into (1) how experience is created and (2) their true identity. *I believe these are the two most valuable things a person can discover:*

- **How experience is created:** We're living in the experience of the principle of THOUGHT taking form in the moment.
- **Our true identity:** Who we really are is CONSCIOUSNESS itself, the wisdom and intelligence behind life.

In each of the case studies that follow, I was working on the basis that the challenge, problem or issue was a result of *believing something that isn't true*, the outside-in misunderstanding. Here's a list of some of the key implications of the 100% inside-out nature of life and what happens when we lose sight of them:

Implication	Explanation	Misunderstanding/Illusion/ Trick of the Mind (When we go outside-in)	The Reality You're Built For/Fact of Life/Pre-existing Truth (When we're awake to the inside-out reality)
You can't be a victim of circumstance.	As you realise you can't be a victim of circumstance, you become less likely to look to the outside for security, approval and validation. Fear of failure and criticism start falling away. It becomes easier to take calculated risks once you know the source of your security and well-being. You become more carefree, enjoying yourself and others as you experiment and explore.	It genuinely seems like we *can* be a victim of circumstance; like a particular experience can harm us psychologically (e.g. giving a talk, being rejected, starting a business, losing a job, being criticised, ending a relationship, getting injured, etc.). While various things can harm us *physically*, nothing can harm you *psychologically*.	We know that we are OK, regardless of how we feel in the moment. We know there's nothing that can harm or damage us psychologically or emotionally. We know that while we may feel uncomfortable sensations from time to time (e.g. worry, anxiety, stress, panic, etc.), they're nothing to be afraid of.
You're wired for realisation: You're an insight machine.	As you come to rely on your innate capacity for realisation, you start trusting that you're going to have the insights you need when you need them. This innate capacity for realisation is the source of innovative solutions to problems. It allows you to see the elusive obvious. Reality is	We overlook the fact that we have the capacity for insight; we innocently believe that we won't have the resources to deal with the situations that we find ourselves in.	We know we have a capacity for insight and realisation that can give us exactly what we need, when we need it. With experience, we come to rely on this capacity more and more.

Implication	Explanation	Misunderstanding/Illusion/ Trick of the Mind (When we go outside-in)	The Reality You're Built For/Fact of Life/Pre-existing Truth (When we're awake to the inside-out reality)
	changing fast, so it can be a relief to discover that you're built to have fresh new perceptions that bring you more closely into alignment with that reality as it evolves.		
We each live in a separate reality.	As you start to see that we each live in our own, THOUGHT-generated perceptual reality, the whole domain of other people gets simpler. You'll start finding it easier to see things from others' perspective – to connect with them and get their world – while staying true to yourself. Your ability to understand what other people are up against lets you identify opportunities, influence with integrity, create solutions and develop strong relationships.	We are more focused on our own thinking and feeling than on other people. We believe that our fears and anxieties are an accurate representation of other people's experience. We are often so preoccupied with our own experience that we are oblivious to other people and their responses.	We find ourselves being curious about other people's experience. We do our best to find out about their perspectives and get their world. We put our attention on them, noticing their responses and adjusting accordingly.

Implication	Explanation	Misunderstanding/Illusion/Trick of the Mind (When we go outside-in)	The Reality You're Built For/Fact of Life/Pre-existing Truth (When we're awake to the inside-out reality)
You're always connected to everyone and everything.	As you realise you're always connected to your true self, to other people and to the whole of life, you discover you're an inherent part of this creative, evolutionary intelligence. The only thing that ever obscures this fact is contaminated thinking arising from the outside-in misunderstanding. As you relax into the truth of this, you become more available to wisdom, realisation and common sense.	We feel isolated from and at the mercy of a world "out there," for example, the past, the future, other people, imagined consequences and outcomes.	We feel connected to other people, to our true selves and to all of life. We notice the ebb and flow of connection as we live our lives. We come to depend on that sense of connection as a reliable signal/guide as we navigate the various situations, circumstances and experiences we find ourselves in.
Your mind is a self-correcting system.	As you continue realising your mind's self-correcting nature, you'll find yourself falling out of contaminated thinking and waking up to reality more and more quickly and easily. As you come to rely on this powerful capacity, you'll spend less time in unnecessary hesitation, worry and	We overlook the fact that our minds are self-correcting, and we innocently believe we need to "do something" to change how we feel and find our way to clarity.	We insightfully realise that we're feeling THOUGHT in the moment, and nothing else. We trust that, while we may feel uncomfortable at times, we can count on our self-correcting minds to give us what we need, when we need it.

Implication	Explanation	Misunderstanding/Illusion/ Trick of the Mind (When we go outside-in)	The Reality You're Built For/Fact of Life/Pre-existing Truth (When we're awake to the inside-out reality)
	conflict. Decision-making becomes easier as you are freed from the misinformation of the outside-in misunderstanding.		
You're built for reality and optimised for results.	You're a born learner, with an extraordinary ability to sense, choose and act. As your understanding of subtractive psychology increases, you become more present and aware, with less on your mind. As a result you find yourself sensing, choosing and acting more fully in alignment with what truly matters to you. This is the path to the kinds of experiences and results truly worth having.	We overlook the fact that we know how to do many things without even thinking about them (e.g. breathing, walking, talking, listening as well as the many specific skills we've each developed). The only thing getting in the way of us being at our best is contaminated thinking arising from the outside-in misunderstanding.	People have been living on this planet for millions of years. We're built for this, and find we can do it effectively and enjoyably when we're not preoccupied with contaminated thinking.

Implication	Explanation	Misunderstanding/Illusion/ Trick of the Mind (When we go outside-in)	The Reality You're Built For/Fact of Life/Pre-existing Truth (When we're awake to the inside-out reality)
Your conception of the future is not reality; now is reality.	While it can be wonderful to envision the future, it doesn't actually exist. Our ideas of the future are not reality; they never include the totality of our innate capacities and of who we really are. As a result, we often overlook a simple fact: *You're built for the reality of the present moment. . . When the future arrives, it will be the present moment. . . The reality you're built for . . . the here and now.*	We mistakenly believe that how we feel when anticipating some future event or occurrence is how we will feel when we're in that situation. We imagine future scenarios then respond to them as though they are an actual reality.	We know that by definition our imagined future scenarios do not include the insights we are going to have in the future. Knowing this, we come to rely on that innate capacity for insight more and more.

In the sections which follow, we'll look at the following topics from a principles perspective and explore case studies for each:

- Fear of public speaking
- Goals, objectives and results
- Social anxiety
- Post-traumatic stress disorder (PTSD)
- Career change
- Stress/stress-related illness
- Burnout
- Relationships
- Depression
- Purpose, direction and navigating by wisdom

Fear of public speaking

Let's look at fear of public speaking through the lens of our seven implications.

- The experience of giving a talk can't harm you psychologically.
- Your capacity for insight can give you exactly what you need, when you need it.
- You can shift your attention from yourself to your audience and their responses.
- As you do, you can start noticing a sense of connection to your listeners.
- Your mind is a self-correcting system, so you don't need to manage how you feel.
- You know how to speak and likely do it most days *without even thinking about it.*
- How you feel when *anticipating* a talk is not equal to how you're going to feel when giving the talk. Your imagined future scenarios do not include the realisations you are going to have in the future.

Case Study

In my book *RESULTS* I wrote about Donna, a woman who was terrified of public speaking and unable to express herself well in large groups. She felt severe anxiety and worried about saying the wrong thing or looking stupid.

Donna had a massive insight while attending my Clarity Certification Training. When I asked her what had happened, she told me, "It's as though a lifetime of limiting beliefs and negative ideas about myself have just fallen away." The experience awakened a passion in Donna to support her peers in the creative industry, and she has gone on to give many talks to groups and conferences. It took courage, but Donna was surprised to discover how easy and enjoyable she found it once she realised she could express herself, free from worry, anxiety and fear.

You can listen to a conversation I had with Donna about her experience here: www.JamieSmart.com/clarity25/Donna

Goals, objectives and results

The whole domain of goals and objectives is one that many people are confused about. Some people claim goals have incredible power, while others say you shouldn't set them at all. Here's a brief excerpt from my book *RESULTS*:

> *A goal is a thought; nothing more. Any feeling you get when you think about a goal is telling you about your THOUGHT-generated perceptual reality in that moment, not about the result you're imagining. While a goal can be a useful tool (e.g. for helping you set a direction, organize your efforts or coordinate the efforts of a group of people), it has no power in and of itself.*

Human beings are naturally goal-oriented. You have an innate capacity for results creation within you. When you have clarity on what you want to create, and are willing to take action, you can learn and adapt as you go. Putting it simply: Clarity plus action equals results.

CLARITY   plus   **ACTION**   equals   **RESULTS**

With that in mind, here are some of the implications that can be particularly relevant when it comes to setting and achieving goals.

- There's nothing that can harm or damage your true identity. This gives you the freedom to follow your heart and take measured risks.
- You don't need to know every step before you can start. You can count on yourself to discover/create the how as you take action and move forward.
- You come from a long line of results creators with the creative power of life within you. As we wake up from the outside-in misunderstanding, what we awaken *to* is a deeper wisdom and intelligence that can guide us.

Case Study (Ten-Year Update)

In Chapter 13, you heard the story of Carl Harvey, who first saw through the hidden hamster wheel trap in relation to a dream convertible he'd just bought. Carl ended up giving the car to his brother as a gift and moving to Australia. Once there, he built his first six-figure business and had his first "mini-retirement" (four-hour work week style).

He quickly realised he didn't want to be retired and his next layer of purpose was unveiled. Carl moved to Malaysia to work for Mind Valley, where he became their top copywriter. While there, he created his first million-dollar business (The Big Life) then moved back to Australia where he created The Abundance Book Club, a company he still runs today.

When I interviewed Carl for the tenth anniversary edition of CLARITY, he said,

I'm still giving away cars. You really did help me realise that it ain't the car that's giving me these thoughts and fears. Now I've got a really healthy balance with money. The idea that that's going to fix me or help me or change me – that's gone. It's just a lovely game to play. And to that extent I've just given my brother a Porsche Truck Turbo-S, my uncle a Mercedes, my auntie a new car, I left a BMW in Australia with my boys, and have just given away another BMW. So one of my goals is never to sell a car, and I've just got a Bentley, so that will be the first true test. It's just a game to demonstrate infinite abundance and zero lack. And it's working really well; people like getting cars. Business is going great, I love what I do, helping lots of people, I got to work with all my heroes. Life is good."

You can listen to a conversation i had with Carl about his experience here: www.Jamiesmart.com/clarity25/Carl

Social anxiety

Various flavours of social anxiety are widespread and have a lot in common with fear of public speaking. The symptoms are feelings of discomfort and awkwardness when in (or thinking about being in) various social situations. But for some people, the effect can be extreme, and can include panic attacks and other physical symptoms such as blushing, sweating and even vomiting. Let's look at some of the implications that are particularly relevant when it comes to social anxiety (you may also like to have another look at the public speaking table).

- You will be OK, regardless of how you feel in the moment. There's nothing that can harm or damage you psychologically or emotionally.
- You have a capacity for realisation that can give you exactly what you need, when you need it. With experience, you'll come to rely on this capacity more and more.
- When you shift your attention from yourself to the people around you, you find yourself being curious about other people. When you do your best to listen deeply and find out about their experience/get their world, you can find yourself feeling more and more connected.
- How you feel when anticipating a social event is not equal to how you're going to feel when you're there. By definition, your THOUGHT-generated future scenarios do not include the realisations you are going to have in the future.

Case Study

Pete had been suffering with extreme social anxiety for many years when I first introduced him to the principles behind clarity. Pete was 19 years old and a member of a group of men to whom I did my very first talk on these principles. After the talk, we listened to a recording by Sydney Banks and I did my best to answer the many questions members of the group had (I was very early in my own exploration of these principles at the time). Pete felt they were interesting ideas but didn't think much more about it.

One evening a few weeks later, Pete was hit with a panic attack while getting ready for a night out with some friends. His thoughts were spiralling as adrenaline flooded his system; the sensations of panic were so severe he actually vomited in the shower. Then, while the warm water ran over his head, he retraced his thoughts and had a sudden insight. . .

You're feeling your own thinking and nothing else.
You've been doing it to yourself!

In a heartbeat, he woke up to the truth of how his experience was being created and his anxiety disappeared. He had a great night out and 13 years later, Pete has gone on to build a successful business and start a family. From time to time, Pete invites me to do a keynote for his employees and when he introduces me, he often shares his own story of insight and describes it as *"one of the most important and pivotal moments of my entire life."*

You can watch a coaching demonstration I did on social anxiety with one of my clients at www.JamieSmart.com/clarity25/Anna

Post-traumatic stress disorder (PTSD)

PTSD is commonly defined as "an anxiety disorder caused by very stressful, frightening or distressing events." But (as we discussed in "What the Research Says" at the end of Chapter 5), researcher and author Marilyn Bowman found that, while the field of psychology assumes a causal connection between adverse events and the experience of trauma, this is not borne out by the research.

The majority of people who experience stressful, frightening or distressing events experience no lasting negative psychological impact from the events (and as discussed at the end of Chapter 15, they can even experience the positive effects of post-traumatic growth).

However, for those who *do* experience PTSD, it can be extremely debilitating. Many sufferers are told that there's no cure – that the best they can hope for is to learn to cope or manage it. But fortunately this is not the case (as you'll see in the following case study).

First, a key distinction: In his excellent book *The Gift of Fear*, security specialist Gavin De Becker explains that true fear is an evolutionary gift; a life-saving response to a potential threat we sense in our *immediate environment*. PTSD, however, is a genuine fear response, but *without* the presence of the threat. While all of these signals are created using the power of THOUGHT in the moment, the thing that distinguishes true fear from PTSD is the presence of a genuine threat in our immediate environment or circumstances.

Case Study

Helen is an army veteran who had been undergoing treatment for PTSD for many years. She had an insight while reading *CLARITY* and everything changed. She wrote to me saying, "I am sure your book *CLARITY* wasn't intended to treat mental illness – but I am a PTSD veteran and it has helped more than psychotherapy and CBT [cognitive behavioural therapy]. I am hopeful again. Thank you."

She explained that she'd been taught various CBT techniques, but that they were most difficult to use at the times she needed them the most. She said, "I've realised that I'm OK. I was diagnosed with PTSD and told there is no cure, but here I am making more strides because of your book than I have in ten years of treatment. Thank you. I am sitting here literally feeling as if I am a fully mentally healthy person. I have never felt that way before."

That was six years ago as I write. Today, Helen is living a happy life and realising her entrepreneurial dreams through the home remodeling business she and her husband now run.

Career change

Making changes in career direction (or any other important decision) can have people feeling stuck and not knowing what to do (or knowing what to do but being afraid to do it). Clarity is your best friend in these situations. As I said in Chapter 19, while inspired action feels great, sometimes you just need to "do the right thing," in spite of your contaminated thinking. As you continue allowing yourself to become more responsive to wisdom, you'll often find that the answers you need come at the exact moment you need them. Remember. . .

- Sometimes the "right thing to do" is to take a specific action.
- Sometimes the "right thing to do" is to stop and take a rest.
- Sometimes the "right thing to do" is to wait for further guidance.

The key is to stay in the game!

Case Study

Emily was working shifts in the National Health System (NHS) on an operating theatre team. She used to daydream about making changes; she wanted to find work that was less stressful and get her weekends back, but she had a secret. While she came across as confident to others, on the inside she was tortured by worry, anxiety and lack of confidence. She was terrified that if she followed her heart it would just be "one more thing to fail at"; she'd been stuck in her job for ten years because she was too scared to leave.

Emily did my Career Transition Blueprint programme, and everything changed. Within four months, she'd left the NHS and started a new job as a professional trainer. She went from working crazy hours, with no spare time and being stressed out of her mind to (1) feeling happy and optimistic, (2) having free time to spend with her friends, and (3) doing a job she loved on a package that was almost *double* her previous salary. She told me, *"I'm happy and I'm not worrying about things. It's quite different to anything that I've had before. I've not had this kind of peace before."*

When I spoke with Emily five years later, she told me that these days, she's willing to make big changes without a second thought. She said, *"The main thing is now when I'm not happy I know I can do something about it and don't feel stuck. There's no fear! Gone are the days of 'What if I can't do it?' or panicking about speaking in front of groups of people. And I never would have had the guts to just start branching out if I hadn't made that initial change! Such a ripple effect!"*

You can listen to a conversation I had with Emily about her experience here: www.JamieSmart.com/clarity25/Emily

Stress/stress-related illness

Stress is one of the most common mental health diagnoses and can show up in a variety of different ways (including emotional, behavioural and physical symptoms). Many addictions and other habitual behaviours are an attempt to reduce the symptoms of stress and restore the system to a place of well-being. As I said in Chapter 7,

The true source of stress is the mistaken belief that we're feeling something other than the principle of THOUGHT taking form in the moment. . .

. . . that we're at the mercy of something other than our moment-to-moment perceptions, a world "out there" in space or time with power over how we feel. . .

Let's look at the subject of stress through the lens of some of the implications we've been exploring. . .

- The feelings of stress and tension are letting you know about the form the creative power of THOUGHT is taking in this moment and nothing else.
- When you *do* feel stressed, you can see it as a signal that points you back in the right direction.
- As you get more and more comfortable feeling uncomfortable, you tap into a greater freedom to navigate the ups and downs of life with ease.

Case Study

Mike had been experiencing dangerously high blood pressure for over 20 years. He said, *"I could break machines! It could go to 225/178 – I should've burst!"* Mike's doctors ran a battery of tests on him before drawing the conclusion that it was stress-related, so he threw everything he could at it: acupuncture, acupressure, various forms of therapy and exercise, but nothing seemed to make a meaningful difference.

Mike didn't tell me any of this before he joined the Clarity Certification Training. The first I knew of it was four months into the programme when Mike announced that his blood pressure had dropped to a healthy range (Mike is in his 60s, so the 140/100 he now operates at is good for his age). Not only had Mike not told me about his stress/blood pressure challenge but he hadn't even been working on *changing* it as he went through the training course. But as he had realisations about the inside-out nature of life, his level of consciousness rose, his stress levels started dropping and his blood pressure followed suit.

And that's one of the beauties of subtractive psychology: a rise in consciousness can eliminate huge amounts of contaminated thinking and take things off your mind *automatically*. Like I said in Chapter 18, a person whose consciousness rises often experiences an "across the board" increase in well-being, with issues they'd been perceiving as problems spontaneously reducing in intensity or even disappearing. Mike said, *"Along with that 'coming home' feeling, my body just relaxed and my stress levels reduced substantially. I recognised what you were pointing to at such a deep level as truth – that my system could let go of thinking the world was a dangerous place. There was no longer a pressure to 'be' anything."*

That was three years ago as I write, and Mike recently confirmed to me that his blood pressure (and stress levels) are still at healthy levels. In fact, things have continued to evolve for him. He told me, *"'Being' now has another meaning to me; not the constructed 'outside-in' being of shoulds, need tos, whens and ifs, but a glimpse of spirit. My spirit, your spirit, our spirit."*

Burnout

Burnout is typically used to describe a set of stress-related symptoms, typically in the domain of work, that leave a person feeling mentally and physically exhausted. When I work with someone who has the symptoms of burnout, they'll often say something like, "I just want things to go back to how they were before I got this." But here's the thing: the symptoms of burnout are typically a *response* to how things were before they got this! Remember the rumble strips from Chapter 5? The person who's been diagnosed with burnout has typically spent months or even years driving on the rumble strips, overriding the signals they've been receiving from their deeper wisdom. But the rumble strips are there for a reason. And as you start to see them for what they are, you allow your system to self-correct, and you find your way back to clarity.

Case Study

Louise O'Dalaigh is a qualified nurse with more than 30 years of experience in health care. She was working in the UK's National Health Service (NHS) when she had her first episode of burnout. She was signed off work for three months, and came back to work after a much-needed rest. Everything seemed fine when a couple of years later, she started to have the symptoms of burnout again.

This time she decided not to leave work and to get to the bottom of it. Her doctor put her on some anti-anxiety medication and she started exploring. She read my *Little Book of Clarity* and had insights and realisations that led to her getting in touch with my company. At the time, her dream was to leave the NHS and start a coaching business, so she enrolled on my Thriving Coaches Blueprint programme. During the kickoff workshop, she had a massive insight that changed her world. She realised deeply that the only thing that's "real" is this moment, that past and future are THOUGHT-generated illusions. She said *"It was like a volcano erupting within me when I realised that I'd been creating my own experience for the past couple of years, replaying the movie over and over again."* She said nobody had ever told her she'd been creating her own experience. It was like a weight being lifted from her, and she suddenly knew she was never going to take anti-anxiety medication again.*

After the workshop, her husband said, *"Even if this is all you ever get from it, it's been worth every penny."* But then something strange happened. She realised that her passion, talent and understanding were desperately needed in the NHS and that she could do the most good right where she was. Today, Louise is the Quality Improvement Lead in her NHS organisation with more than 10,000 staff, and she's working in a variety of ways to support well-being within her organisation. Louise also went on to train as a Certified Clarity Coach and has a number of coaching clients inside and outside of her organisation. Recently she was invited to give the keynote speech at the world's largest 3 Principles conference. She said, *"When I spoke at the 3PUK conference, I described my transformative journey like moving from Velcro to Teflon . . . things don't stick to me anymore. I just let them go. There are so many things I'm involved in, so many ongoing challenges both in work and outside of it but I'm not carrying the weight of them."* Louise is also a mother of four children, so it's not just her that's been helped by this understanding. She said, *"The impact this has had on me personally, my family and many many colleagues is something that money just can't buy."*

* Louise realised that she no longer needed to take medication. When someone starts getting a deeper understanding of these principles, it's not unusual for their medication requirements to reduce or even disappear. However, if you're on a prescription, it's essential that you consult your doctor or psychiatrist before changing your dosage or stopping your medication.

You can listen to a conversation I had with Louise about her experience here: www.JamieSmart.com/clarity25/Louise

Relationships

Relationships are important for almost every aspect of our lives, and most of us have many people we're in relationship with. Relationships can be beautiful sources of love, learning and laughter. But perhaps it's not surprising that something so universal can also be a source of frustration, confusion and conflict. The Clarity Relationship Quadrant helps bring some light to this often-confusing area.

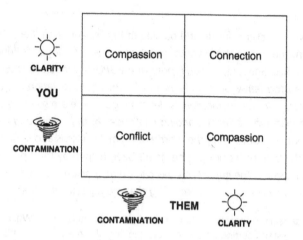

The Clarity Relationship Quadrant is very simple. It works on these premises:

- Your feelings are always letting you know about THOUGHT taking form in your experience, moment to moment.
- Other people will appear to be consistent with your THOUGHT-generated perceptual reality.
- When neither participant has clarity, it's a recipe for conflict.
- When one person in a relationship has clarity, it creates space for the other person to start finding clarity, too.

This is incredibly encouraging news; it means that clarity in your relationships starts with you. Let's look at the quadrant in a little more detail. . .

1. **The Zone of Conflict:** When two or more people are caught in contaminated thinking, conflict is a strong possibility. It will genuinely seem to each party like their uncomfortable feelings are being caused by the other party(ies).

2. **The Zone of Connection:** When two or more people have clarity, love and connection are a strong possibility. It will genuinely seem to each party like their beautiful feelings are being caused by the other party(ies).

3. and 4. **The Zones of Compassion:** When one person is caught in contaminated thinking, it may seem like their uncomfortable feelings are being caused by the other person. But if that other person has clarity, they will quickly see that their colleague is lost, and their heart will go out to them. They will be full of compassion, and the person with contaminated thinking may even feel that. Either way, by bringing clarity to the relationship, you avoid getting into the kinds of negative feedback loops that can quickly escalate into conflict.

Case Study (Ten-Year Update)

In Chapter 16, you heard about Ian whose understanding of the principles behind clarity made a big difference in his role as a programme manager. When I spoke with Ian for the tenth anniversary edition of *CLARITY*, he explained that this understanding didn't just help create a good feeling and high performance in his teams; it's also had a big impact in his life as a whole. He said, *"I was looking for something to elevate me, and once I was pointed in the right direction, everything slotted into place. I got a sliver of knowing, and that one thing has elevated things ever since."*

Ian still works in a fast-moving environment with lots of ups and downs. While he's tenacious and driven, he said his career has "looked after itself." He says he still sometimes feels frustrated, but there's a calmness behind the scenes that allows him to focus on people and relationships. Ian used to "overthink" outside of work, and he suffered from insomnia, but that's really changed, too. He still gets insomnia from time to time, but now it's without the racing thoughts. He said, *"Before clarity, I used to let it be a problem, but my thinking doesn't get really loud these days, so it doesn't bother me."* Ian told me that the key was the subtractive nature of this understanding. He said, *"You need to take things away. It's quite hard to describe but it's really been transformative to my life."*

Depression

Depression is an extremely common mental health diagnosis. While it has been popular to attribute it to "chemical imbalances" the validity of that model is now being called into question. As I wrote in *RESULTS*:

> . . . *a 2013 paper by Brett J. Deacon, PhD (published in the highly regarded* Clinical Psychology Review: The Future of Evidence-Based Practice in Psychotherapy) *raises significant concerns about the biomedical model. He suggests that framing mental disorders as biochemically induced brain diseases, then treating them with "disease-specific" psychiatric medications has led to a lack of clinical innovation, and poor results for patients. Deacon states that "an honest and public dialog about the validity and utility of the biomedical paradigm is urgently needed."*

> *Source:* Deacon, B. J. (2013). The biomedical model of mental disorder: A critical analysis of its validity, utility, and effects on psychotherapy research. *Clinical Psychology Review, 33(7),* 846–861.

Case Study

Robin had been struggling with depression for many years and was already on medication when the global financial crisis hit in 2008. The depression got worse, and over the next couple of years, his wife left him and Robin had to shut down his company. To his credit, Robin managed to place all his employees in new jobs before he closed the doors on the business (a truck dealership). He was able to take satisfaction from that, but the depression persisted, so he started looking for a way out.

In the years that followed, Robin trained in NLP, hypnosis, did a postgraduate degree in leadership and earned his ILM 7 (an advanced qualification) from the Institute of Leadership and Management. While the courses helped with Robin's business (he was working as a trainer and consultant), none of it helped with the depression. He explained, *"My demons kept coming back, and I just couldn't find a way out."*

Then Robin read the first edition of CLARITY. He told me, *"To be honest it didn't make a lot of sense, but I thought maybe it could help me anyway."* He started exploring the materials on my website and decided to come on my Thriving Coaches Blueprint programme. Three weeks into the programme, he stopped taking his medication; Robin told me, *"Something shifted inside me, and I suddenly realised 'I don't need these anymore.'"* The next few months were a bumpy ride as he adjusted to living without medication.*

When I spoke with Robin recently, he told me, *"The profound thing for me is that this didn't stop the feelings, but I don't have depression. I just need to find a quiet place when those feelings come. These days, within 30–60 minutes, I'm fine."* Robin now relates to those feelings as a signal, letting him know when he needs to look in a different direction. *"I now know it's me that's doing it, so I can change it. I can let it be, and take myself to the place where it isn't."*

* As with Louise, Robin also realised that he no longer needed to take medication. However, please remember that if you're on a prescription, it's essential that you consult your doctor or psychiatrist before changing your dosage or stopping your medication.

Purpose, direction and navigating by wisdom

More and more people are preoccupied with the search for purpose and meaning in life. But how do you actually "find your purpose"? The subtractive nature of the inside-out understanding gives us a more valuable question to ask, "What gets in the way of your realising purpose?" What gets in the way is looking for it where it isn't. . .

> *The misguided search for purpose
> is the biggest obstacle to finding it.*

When the fog of contaminated "I'll be happy when. . ." thinking is blown away, what remains is the clarity that shines from the heart of your being. Like the sun behind the clouds, it's always there.

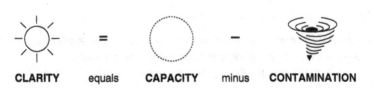

CLARITY   equals   **CAPACITY**   minus   **CONTAMINATION**

If we look at purpose and direction through the lens of implications, we find that there's quite a bit of overlap with the previously described Goals.

Case Study (Ten-Year Update)

In Chapter 12, you heard the story of Jack and Vivienne, who discovered a passion for soap making. Here's what happened next: In 2013, they moved to France where they quickly discovered that, while people loved their soap, they would need to manufacture a huge amount of it to make a decent living. This would mean industrialising, a move which didn't fit with the kind of lives they wanted to live, so they pivoted.

Over the next few years, they followed their wisdom, going for what they really wanted and "doing what made sense" each step of the way. They bought into a real estate franchise and had a great time exploring the French countryside, meeting new people and finding new places (they also discovered how much they love living in the Pyrenees!). But over time, they started to see that the people running the franchise didn't share their values. One day they woke up and realised, "We don't have to do this. We can stop!" That brought them to their next experiment – running an Airbnb in the French countryside – where they met lots of lovely people and made some lasting friendships.

Today, Jack and Viv still love making soap for their customers. Viv also coaches and writes books, while Jack has officially retired and is currently renovating a house in the valley they describe as their "spiritual home" (in fact, the story of how they *found* that home is an object lesson in wisdom and synchronicity). Vivienne said: *"You look back at the way your life goes and you see the times when you've listened to whatever that is – wisdom or whatever you want to call it – the times when you've actually followed that, and how things have worked out."*

> When I asked them what difference understanding the principles behind clarity had made to them, Vivienne said, *"It's changed everything . . . how I think about people, how I relate to people. It's made it so much easier to ride the waves and be in our life. We've got a beautiful life. We love our life."*

Of the ten examples described in this chapter, many of them would be classed as "disorders" (e.g. depression, anxiety disorder, PTSD, etc.). The American Psychiatric Association's *Diagnostic and Statistical Manual* (aka the *DSM V*) lists *100s* of mental disorders. There are nearly *1000* different schools of intervention-based therapy (e.g. CBT, Jungian, psychodynamic, Freudian, psychospiritual, NLP, positive psychology, hypnotherapy, etc.). Each propose different "causes" for these disorders, and offer a wide variety of solutions.

Meanwhile, new disorders are "discovered" each year. Babies are born with sound mental health, but society is turning them into "mentally ill" teenagers and adults at an unprecedented rate. Diagnoses of anxiety and depression are on the increase, and stressed-out Western doctors are prescribing more psychiatric medication than ever before. Remember that passage from the book *Discovery of the Germ* that I shared in the Preface?

> *In just 20 years, the central role of germs in producing illness was for the first time decisively demonstrated and Western doctors abandoned misconceived ideas about the causes and nature of disease that had persisted, in one form or another, for thousands of years.*

Are you open to the possibility that the field of psychology today is in a similar position to where the field of medicine was in the nineteenth century? Is it possible that we could discover something that would have psychologists, psychiatrists and medical doctors *abandon misconceived ideas about the causes and nature of mental health issues that have persisted, in one form or another, for thousands of years?*

*The discovery of the principles behind clarity is to
psychology what the discovery of germs was to medicine.*

You may recall my personal mission is to awaken people and help them awaken others. As I write, I've spent the past 14 years coaching, teaching and doing therapeutic change work with thousands of clients *using these principles exclusively*. I've road tested the principles behind clarity in my own work and trained thousands of coaches, therapists and change workers to do the same. As the years have passed, the truth of these principles has become clearer and simpler to me, and the impact of my work has continued to increase. The same is true of the results my colleagues and students are getting with *their* clients.

As I wrote in the Preface, the world has changed radically since CLARITY was first published. As we reach the end of this new edition, it seems to me that there are two main reasons why the world needs this understanding more than ever before:

1. **Well-being:** We're facing a humanitarian crisis in mental health, and the field is buckling under the strain of trying to operate without knowing the foundational principles that underpin it.
2. **Wisdom:** Our habits of thinking have not developed for the exponential world we're now living in. We need wisdom, compassion and exponential insight to meet the challenges of the digital age.

In Chapter 22, I quoted Dee Ward Hock saying that a 400-year-old age is dying and another is struggling to be born. The challenges of well-being and wisdom are a part of those birth struggles, and the principles we're exploring are part of the solution. The only qualification you need to share this understanding are your own insights and the feeling you're living in. And as my dear friend, colleague and mentor Chip Chipman once said. . .

The feeling you're living in is all you get.

Keep exploring ❖ connect with others
share your discoveries ❖ deepen your understanding

Thought Experiment: *Have you already started to notice that any lingering sense you may have had that there's somewhere to get to (and that there is better than here) was an illusion? That the search is over?*

What the Research Says: At the end of Chapter 18, I mentioned an interview I did with my good friend and colleague, Dr William (Bill) F. Pettit. He's a board-certified psychiatrist and has been working with the principles described in this book exclusively for nearly 40 years. Dr Pettit has treated tens of thousands of patients, with diagnoses as diverse as schizophrenia, depression, bipolar disorder, stress, panic attacks and many more conditions.

Dr Pettit and I recorded a two-hour conversation where we explored the kinds of issues mentioned in this chapter as well as schizophrenia, bipolar disorder and many others. We also answered questions from my community about the impact of this understanding. Our conversation was full of illuminating examples and fascinating stories from Bill's casebook.

You can find the interview at www.JamieSmart.com/research/Clarity25

Acknowledgements

....

The author's name is on the cover, but there are always others without whom a book would never see the light of day. Countless people have contributed to me, my learning and my work over the years. I will never be able to fully thank them all. However, there are a number of people whose support and guidance have been integral to the creation of this book. Special thanks go to. . .

All my teachers, colleagues, clients and readers, past and present. . .

The pioneering community of Clarity Coaches, Consultants, Trainers, Facilitators and Practitioners who are with me on this adventure. . .

The people who have so generously allowed me to tell their stories in this book. . .

The team at Capstone, for your support and expertise. . .

The team at Clarity Academy Ltd, past and present, for your care and creativity (and to Clesia, Deb, Dzidek, Emma, Eugenia and Morena specifically for helping keep the wheels turning while I worked on this tenth anniversary edition). . .

Christina Hall, PhD, for the magic of language and an open heart. . .

Chip and Jan Chipman, for your friendship, love and understanding. . .

Tilly, Boo and all my family, my heart is filled with gratitude and love for you. . .

My darling Emma McDevitt, for everything. . .

And finally, to Sydney Banks, for uncovering the principles behind clarity and sharing them with the world.

Discover Your Clarity Quotient

Here's how you can start accelerating your results now: Discover your personal Clarity Quotient by answering 20 simple questions (multiple choice). This quick and easy questionnaire gives you a snapshot of your current state of mind, including a stress score and an engagement score, plus suggestions for how you can improve your score quickly and easily.

You can discover your clarity quotient for free at

www.jamiesmart.com/CQ

The Clarity Self-Coaching Programme

Get free access and continue your journey with
the principles behind clarity. . .

Are you open to the possibility that the keys to you living your most inspiringly beautiful life reside at the heart of your being? The CLARITY Self-Coaching Programme is a powerful, eight-part journey to transform your life, focusing on these key areas:

- Success
- Relationships
- Money
- Health
- Work
- Purpose
- Results
- Freedom

The CLARITY Self-Coaching Programme is one of our best-selling self-study courses. To celebrate the tenth anniversary edition of *CLARITY*, we've decided to make this life-changing programme available at no charge to readers of this book who want to continue their clarity journey.

You can **get free access** now at

www.JamieSmart.com/transform

Clarity for Coaches, Therapists, Trainers and Facilitators

Jamie Smart is passionate about supporting transformation professionals (e.g. coaches, trainers, consultants, therapists, facilitators, etc.) in bringing the principles behind clarity into their work with clients, into their own businesses and into their lives.

If you're passionate about making a difference, Jamie has a variety of programmes serving the growing community of transformation professionals who are leveraging the principles behind clarity in their work with clients and growing their practices. These include virtual courses, 1:1 coaching and the Clarity Certification Programmes.

All these programmes are oriented around the three essential transformations you need to share this understanding at a professional level: (1) grounding – deepening your embodied understanding of these principles; (2) impact – increasing your ability to share this understanding with others; and (3) leverage – discovering the keys to making your living from the inside out and taking your practice or business to the next level. These programmes are also popular with entrepreneurs, business owners and other leaders who want to bring an understanding of these principles into their work and their lives.

If you're a transformation professional and want to take things to a new level, here's what to do next:

1. Download the book *The Thriving Coaches Scorecard* to identify your sticking points, leverage points and quick wins for taking your grounding, impact and practice to a new level. It's a quick read with a powerful effect, and you can get it for free at

www.JamieSmart.com/scorecard

2. Join the Thriving Coaches Group on Facebook and connect with the growing community of like-minded transformation professionals who are passionate about exponentially increasing their grounding, impact and their livelihood. You can join for free at

www.JamieSmart.com/thriving

3. Listen to the *Thriving Coaches* podcast for free at

www.JamieSmart.com/TCP

For details of the Clarity Certification Programmes go to

www.JamieSmart.com/professional

Clarity
for Businesses
and Other
Organisations

....

Jamie Smart and his team work with a variety of businesses ranging from an SME ranked as one of the *Sunday Times'* 100 Best Small Companies to Work For to a Fortune 500 business designated by Ethisphere as one of the world's most ethical companies. Jamie Smart has keynoted conferences for organisations ranging from Hewlett Packard and Dun & Bradstreet to the Nato Defense College and the Council of the Institute and Faculty of Actuaries. Some of the services we offer:

- Keynote speeches on a variety of topics
- Mental clarity for performance and well-being
- Cultivating a results mindset
- Leadership in a rapidly changing world
- Resilience in times of uncertainty
- Coaching for well-being, performance and results

- Executive coaching and 1:1 intensives
- Teambuilding workshops and leadership retreats
- Consulting projects to solve specific business issues
- In-house coaching and coach-training programmes

To find out if your organisation is a good fit for a Clarity project, get in touch with us on **business@jamiesmart.com**

Subtractive Psychology

Subtractive psychology is a term coined by Jamie Smart to refer to the radical new approach to resilience, well-being and mental health described in this book. It is being used with dramatic results (under a variety of names by leading-edge practitioners) in domains as diverse as elite sports, blue-chip companies, treatment centres, business startups and even the penal system.

The power of subtractive psychology lies in its simplicity: The field is grounded in the discovery (by the philosopher Sydney Banks) that there are principles that govern human psychology, just as there are fundamental principles that govern the natural world. As an individual develops an embodied understanding of the principles behind clarity, they start to see through conditioned psychological habits such as stress, worry and anxiety.

This understanding is (as the name suggests) entirely subtractive, taking things off people's minds and allowing their innate capacities to come to the fore. As a person has less on their mind, their innate resilience, well-being and peace of mind shine through more fully and effortlessly allowing them the freedom to experience life to the full, flourish and thrive.

www.SubtractivePsychology.com

About Jamie Smart

Jamie Smart is a *Sunday Times* bestselling author, educator, speaker and coach who presents regularly at major conferences worldwide. He shows individuals and organisations the unexpected keys to clarity, the ultimate leverage point for creating profound transformation and meaningful results.

Jamie's primary focus is in showing business leaders, entrepreneurs, coaches, therapists and other transformation professionals how to bring subtractive psychology and the principles behind clarity into their work with clients, into their own businesses and into every aspect of their lives. In addition, he works with a handful of 1:1 coaching clients and leads selected corporate programmes.

Jamie has keynoted conferences for organisations ranging from the NATO Defense College to the mental health charity, Rethink Mental Illness and the Council of the Institute and Faculty of Actuaries. His corporate clients range from household names like Hewlett Packard and Dun & Bradstreet to The Specialist Works, an SME ranked as one of the *Sunday Times*'s 100 Best Small Companies to Work For. He has appeared on Sky TV and on the BBC, as well as in numerous publications including *The Times*, *The Daily Telegraph*, *The Huffington Post* and *Psychologies Magazine*. As well as *CLARITY* he is also the author of the books *RESULTS: Think Less, Achieve More*, *The Little Book of Clarity* and *The Little Book of Results*.

Jamie lives in the UK. When he's not working, he loves spending time with his family, travelling, walking, drinking coffee and exploring.

You can connect with Jamie on the following social media sites:

Instagram:	@JamieSmartCom
Twitter:	@JamieSmartCom
Facebook:	www.Facebook.com/jamiesmartcom
YouTube:	www.youtube.com/clarityjamiesmart
LinkedIn:	https://www.linkedin.com/in/ JamieSmartClarity

You can read Jamie's blog, get full contact details and find his podcasts at the link below or wherever you get your podcasts.

www.JamieSmart.com

Index